THE FUTURE OF PAROLE

The Future of PAROLE

Commentaries on systems in Britain and U.S.A.

Edited by D. J. WEST
Lecturer in Criminology and Fellow of Darwin College, Cambridge
Foreword by Lord Hunt
Chairman of the Parole Board

DUCKWORTH

First published in 1972 by Gerald Duckworth &
Company Limited, 3 Henrietta Street, London, W.C.2.

Cloth ISBN 0 7156 0610 7

Paper ISBN 0 7156 0635 2

Printed by Bristol Typesetting Co. Ltd.,
Barton Manor, St Philips, Bristol.

Contents

Contributors 6

Foreword *Lord Hunt* 7

Editor's preface 9

1 Parole in England: an introductory explanation *D. J. West* 11

2 Parole in England: some comments on the system at work *D. J. West* 21

3 The Local Review Committee *J. P. Martin* 32

4 Caring for offenders on parole *W. H. Pearce* 58

5 Parole philosophy in England and America *Evelyn Shea* 66

6 Some consequences of a parole system for prison management *Keith Hawkins* 96

7 Parole for the ex-prisoner: carrot, stick or illusion? *J. Irvin Waller* 116

8 The assessment of risk in parole decision making *Vincent O'Leary and Daniel Glaser* 135

Notes 199

Index 209

CONTRIBUTORS

DANIEL GLASER A.M., PH.D.
Department of Sociology and Anthropology, University of Southern California

KEITH HAWKINS LL.B., Dipl. Criminol., M.A., PH.D.
Fellow of Gonville and Caius College, Cambridge

J. P. MARTIN M.A., PH.D.
Professor of Social Administration, University of Southampton

VINCENT O'LEARY M.A.
Professor of Criminal Justice, State University of New York at Albany

W. H. PEARCE O.B.E.
Principal Probation Officer, London Probation and After-Care Service (formerly member of the Parole Board of England)

EVELYN SHEA LL.D. (Basel), Dipl. Criminol.
Ottawa, Canada

J. IRVIN WALLER M.A., Dipl. Criminol.
Research Associate, Toronto University Centre of Criminology

D. J. WEST M.D., PH.D., M.R.C. Psych.
Lecturer in Criminology and Fellow of Darwin College, Cambridge (formerly member of the Parole Board of England)

Foreword

Parole, as defined by Dr West in the opening chapter of this book, was grafted on to the British penal system late in time, in contrast with a number of other countries, where methods of granting conditional release at some stage during a fixed-term prison sentence have been practised for many years; the legislation embodying this measure was, as he has explained, placed upon the Statute Book in the British Parliament less than five years ago, during the life of the previous Parliament. It was acclaimed as an enlightened measure during the debates in both Houses and, as a parliamentarian who knew too little at that time about criminal law and penal practices, I was persuaded of its potential prospects by the fact that the relevant clauses in the Bill were considered constructively by nearly all Members qualified to speak on this matter, irrespective of political allegiance.

In giving due credit to the former Government for introducing parole, I would like to pay a personal tribute to the late Lord Stonham. His devotion to the cause of prison reform has lately been given public recognition, following his untimely death, and as the responsible Minister in the Home Office at the time, it was only natural that the parole scheme should have been dear to him. Having worked close to him as the first Chairman of the Parole Board for England and Wales, I am glad to testify to the faith and enthusiasm of Victor Stonham in the task of proving its value, and to express my gratitude for the encouragement he gave me in the early days.

In accepting a heavy responsibility, those of us who were invited to play our part, as members of the Board, in launching the scheme were also granted a great privilege. There was the challenge of pioneering an important project and of helping to steer it successfully through its formative years. There was the infectious hope that it contained the seeds of significant social advance. There was, and will remain, the need to develop a special skill, compounded of a wide conspectus of experience and of sound judgment, in making assessments on the issue of releasing into the community, at the optimum point in time, people who, whether because of some personal inadequacy or because of a latent criminality, stand in need of supervision and support in order to enhance their prospects of abiding by the law in the future.

Such a task will always involve an element of risk for law-abiding members of the community during the process of rehabilitation. Whenever a further and serious offence is committed during parole it is natural that there should be public anxiety. This concern is equally felt by the Parole Board and it is most important to review the reasons for the advice which was given to the Home Secretary in all such cases. But it is no less important to maintain a sense of proportion in regard to the system as a whole. It may serve the public interest no better to be generally over-cautious than to move too fast towards a wider application of parole. The essence of the problem is to balance the probable advantages of a phased and controlled rehabilitation against the risks in each particular case; to bear in mind the eventual danger of releasing the offender at the end of his sentence without any mandate to impose supervision or provide support.

For this task it is a source of strength and comfort to be supported by enlightened and experienced colleagues. Among the pioneers was Donald West, from whom I learned much and to whom I am glad of the opportunity to express my gratitude publicly. He has now rendered a further considerable service by drawing together the threads stemming from a number of national systems of conditional early release which the authors of the British parole system had the advantage of studying beforehand and which members of my Board have since observed during our visits. All these systems despite their differences have in common a simple thesis: the burden of responsibility upon us all, both to improve the social conditions which give rise to many crimes and to apply such constructive remedies as befit an enlightened society, to those who commit them.

LORD HUNT of Llanfair Waterdine
Chairman, The Parole Board
December 1971

Editor's preface

This collection of essays about parole is concerned in the first instance with the system as it has developed in recent years in England. Many of the principles involved, and the problems that arise, are common to parole systems everywhere. The later chapters have been written by authors who have studied parole systems in the United States and Canada, but their comments are also relevant to what happens in England.

The first chapter is a brief statement about the nature of the English parole system, and this is followed by a second chapter commenting upon how the system appears to be working out in practice and how it might possibly be improved.

The third chapter considers in greater detail what is probably the most important sector of the parole selection system, the Local Review Committees at the prisons. They consider every eligible case and make the first selection of suitable candidates. The fourth chapter, written by a member of the probation service who was also a member of the English Parole Board, deals with the crucial question of the provision of appropriate supervision for those who are released on parole.

The fifth chapter is of a more theoretical nature and covers the legal philosophy underlying parole as revealed in the drafting of statutes. This is written by a lawyer who has made a special study of the differences between England and the United States in this respect. The sixth chapter, written by a criminologist who has carried out an extensive research into American parole systems, explores the relation between parole and prison, and the effect of parole on the penal system generally.

The seventh chapter deals with the most fundamental question of all, namely the effectiveness or otherwise of parole supervision as a means of preventing crime or helping offenders. It is written by a research worker who is at present busily engaged on a large project of research into parole in Canada. The problems of evaluating effectiveness discussed in that chapter apply with equal force in every country. Whether the author's somewhat depressingly sceptical conclusions will be found to apply to parole supervision in England remains to be seen. Comparable research findings are not yet available in England, but the Home Office Research Unit is working on this problem, and some preliminary results suggest that offenders granted parole have a reduced liability to reconviction. (See Appendix 3, *Report of the Parole Board for 1970*, HMSO, July 1971.)

The eighth and final chapter is written by two American authorities. Vincent O'Leary, now a professor of criminal justice, was previously Director of the National Parole Institutes, and before that had pursued a distinguished career in parole services. Dr Glaser, a distinguished sociologist who has specialised in penology, was at one time a sociologist actuary with the Illinois Parole and Pardon Board. Their contribution deals with the primary function of all parole boards, namely selection for release in relation to risk of failure on parole. They bring to the topic a wide knowledge of the practical outcome of various selection policies and methods of helping parolees. In the course of their essay, they make many practical observations which, besides being of considerable general interest, cannot fail to be of help to the decision makers. Even so, a certain amount of uncertainty and subjectivity inevitably remains, and the chapter ends with a plea for more experiment and more careful recording of results.

1 Parole in England: an introductory explanation

D. J. WEST

What is parole?

Parole, as it is understood in the United Kingdom, is a procedure whereby a sentence imposed by a court of justice may be varied by administrative action. Carefully selected inmates may be let out of prison in advance of their expected date of release, but on condition that they agree to accept supervision by a probation officer and that they understand they are still under sentence and liable to recall to prison if they misbehave. The system was set up under the Criminal Justice Act, 1967, and the first releases on parole took place on 1 April 1968.

The parole system is not to be confused with remission for good behaviour. English prisoners are normally released to complete freedom when they have completed two thirds of the term fixed by the judge when sentencing, provided that they do not forfeit any part of their remission time as a punishment for misconduct or lose time as a consequence of ill-advised appeals. Thus, a sentence of (say) three years means in effect two years, but with an almost never enforced theoretical possibility of a maximum of three years in prison. Parole is therefore an additional provision enabling a prisoner to be released under supervision before two thirds of his sentence is up.

The Criminal Justice Act specifies that parole may not be granted before a prisoner has completed one third of his sentence or one year, whichever is the longer. This stipulation means that parole applies only to prisoners with sentences of more than eighteen months. The period under compulsory supervision for ordinary prisoners runs from the date of actual release up to the date when they would normally have been released, given one third remission, had no parole been granted. Thus a prisoner serving three years or longer, who is released on parole immediately he becomes eligible, spends the first third of his sentence in prison, the second third out of prison but under supervision and liable to recall, and the final third as a completely free man. Young prisoners under twenty-one at the time of sentence, and recidivists given 'extended' sentences are exceptions to these rules. They are subject to compulsory supervision up to the very end of their sentence whether or not they are granted early release on parole.

Nor must parole under the Criminal Justice Act be confused with temporary leave of absence from prison, which is sometimes referred to loosely as 'parole'. This is occasionally granted for compassionate reasons (for instance, to attend a funeral or visit a dying relative) or may be given to prisoners shortly before their date of release so that they can make arrangements about work or accommodation, or prepare the way for a return to their families. Finally, parole must not be confused with other pre-existing schemes of partial release. Some long-term prisoners in the last stages of their sentence, for instance, are allowed out during working hours, so that they can begin employment, although they must return each evening to the prison or to a hostel attached to the prison. These other schemes apply to restricted categories of prisoners, and are operated entirely at the discretion of the Prison Department of the Home Office. Parole, however, is a release procedure for which all prisoners except those serving eighteen months or less must be considered. Moreover, except for the very few instances in which the Home Secretary exercises his legal right to veto release, the granting of parole rests with authorities who can act independently of Home Office departments.

The authorities who grant parole.

All eligible prisoners are considered for parole unless they say they are unwilling. They cannot be forced into agreement. The term parole comes from the French for 'word of honour', and implies that the prisoner agrees of his own volition to be of good behaviour if granted release.

In the first instance, the candidates are considered by the Local Review Committee at the prison where the offender is being held. These committees are composed of the prison governor (or his representative) and not less than three other persons, who are appointed by the Home Secretary. None of these other persons may be an officer of the prison, but one of them must be a probation officer, and another must be one of the Board of Visitors of the prison. These committees are expected to meet and consider every case in good time before the earliest date of eligibility for release on parole. The deliberations are based primarily upon a reading of the offender's case history in the prison file; but in addition one of the committee (other than the governor) must see the prisoner beforehand and put to the meeting any oral representations which the prisoner wants him to convey. The Review Committees are also required to take into account any written representation which the prisoner wishes to make.

With certain exceptions, which are mentioned later, if a Local Review Committee rejects an application, that normally closes the matter. However, the rejected prisoner must be considered again annually, until either he gets parole or he is discharged from prison in the normal way. Occasionally Review Committees suggest that a prisoner should be considered again in less than a year's time.

In practice, parole is regarded as something of a privilege and is granted to only a minority of candidates. Since most of the rejections occur at the Local Review stage, these Committees have the major role in the selection of offenders for release on parole. The operation of the Review Committee is described in further detail in a later chapter, but it might be pointed out here that the presence of the prison governor on these bodies, often in the capacity of chairman, ensures that the view of the prison authorities receives, to put it mildly, a great deal of weight.

When the Local Review Committee has reached a decision, its recommendation, together with a brief outline of reasons for its decision, are forwarded with the case dossier to the Home Office Parole Unit. If there is disagreement between members of the Review Committee, a minority statement, also giving reasons, accompanies the papers. All cases that are favourably recommended by a Local Review Committee are automatically put before the Parole Board.

The Parole Unit of the Home Office receives the dossiers from the Local Review Committees, checks the legality and timing of parole procedures, checks on missing documentation and seeks any additional information likely to be wanted by the Board. It also brings to the notice of the officials concerned any cases in which the Home Secretary might wish to exercise his veto in the event of the Board recommending parole. It checks when offenders who have been accomplices become eligible for parole, and assembles their dossiers so that the Board can review together all who have been involved in the same crime, even though they may not all have been recommended by the Local Review Committee. The Parole Unit also identifies all cases in which the risk of reconviction within two years is calculated to be less than 35 per cent, and puts all such cases to the Board whether or not they have been recommended by Review Committees.

The Parole Board is a body appointed by the Home Secretary to advise him on parole, and the selection of persons to serve on the Board is entirely at his discretion. Apart from the salaried Chairman (Lord Hunt of mountaineering fame) the members undertake Parole Board duties in addition to their ordinary work, receiving attendance fees and expenses. This arrangement ensures that the Board is served by knowledgeable persons most of whom are actively engaged in various branches of legal or penal practice. The Criminal Justice Act (Schedule II) lays down that the Board shall include a member of the judiciary, a psychiatrist, a person with experience in the supervision and after-care of offenders, and a person who has studied the causes of delinquency or the treatment of offenders. The last two categories have generally been filled by a probation officer and an academic criminologist. The lay or independent members have included some with very relevant qualifications, for example a retired Chief Constable, a prison visitor, and a comprehensive school head-mistress. Initially, in addition to the chairman, the Board consisted of 16 members, including two or three in each of the four statutory categories. It has since been expanded several times in order to cope with the increasing number of cases referred to it. At present, in 1971, there are 33 members. Most members are asked to serve for up to three years or sometimes longer.

The Board divides itself up into panels of about six for the purpose of considering cases. In 1971 about three panel meetings are being held every week, one of which normally meets outside London in Birmingham or Manchester. The Parole Unit sends copies of the case dossiers to every member in advance of their date of meeting, so the members can familiarise themselves with the facts of each case before discussion and decision-making begins. If opinion is seriously divided, a case may be put back for reconsideration by another panel, or by a meeting of the whole Board. The decision of a Parole Board panel takes the form of a recommendation to the Home Secretary on three points: (1) Whether the offender should be released on parole; (2) The date of release; (3) The conditions to be written into the parole licence.

The Home Office nearly always accepts and acts upon these recommendations promptly. Certain cases, however, are liable to be referred for consideration by a Minister or by the Home Secretary himself. There are no fixed rules as to which types of prisoner these are, but it is reasonable to assume that they include cases in which political or security considerations arise, those that have achieved public notoriety, and those involving serious crimes of a violent or sexual nature.

The final responsibility for parole in England thus rests with the Home Secretary. Although he cannot release an offender on parole without a recommendation from the Board, he is under no obligation to follow the Board's advice when release is proposed. The Local Review Committees and the Board itself are composed of individuals selected by the Home Secretary, and some of these individuals (in particular the probation officers) belong to services run by the Home Office. Any serious possibility of a conflict of aims between the Board and the Home Secretary would seem unlikely to arise, although in practice the individuals selected are independent-minded and far from being 'yes men'.

Since the Board is only an advisory body, the Home Secretary does not have to refer a case for consideration unless he sees fit. When parole was introduced the Parole Unit in the Home Office at first used its own discretion on behalf of the Home Secretary as to what cases to refer to the Parole Board. Of the thousand or so prisoners who became eligible on 1 April 1968 and were favourably recommended by Local Review Committees, nearly five hundred were not considered suitable by the Home Office, and were never put before the Board. Early in its life the English Parole Board (though not its counterpart in Scotland) expressed concern about this procedure. In due course the Home Secretary in England decided to seek his Board's views in all cases in which Local Review Committees had made a recommendation for release. Had he not come to this decision, it could have been argued that the Board was being used merely to give formal approval to decisions reached by Home Office officials. The Scottish Home and Health Department, however, continued to function as a supplementary review body, rejecting or adding to the cases recommended by Review Committees before referral to the Parole Board for Scotland.

Another change of procedure was announced in July 1969.[1] Until then it had been the practice for Home Office officials to warn the Board whenever a case came up which was of a kind in which the Home Secretary might wish to exercise his power of veto. Thereafter, the Home Secretary decided to abandon this practice, and to postpone his own consideration of cases until after the Board had deliberated and made a recommendation. This was obviously a better way to obtain an independent opinion from the Board.

Conditions of parole

The parolee is not an entirely free man. He comes out of prison on a licence into which is written certain standard conditions. He must report without delay to the officer named in the licence and place himself under supervision. He must 'be of good behaviour and lead an industrious life'. The Home Office, in a pamphlet of advice to prisoners[2] explains that this means 'do your level best to get a job and try to keep it'. If a parolee fails to report to his supervising officer, or fails to give his correct address or place of work, he is obviously not fulfilling the expected conditions. The Home Office pamphlet goes on to explain to prisoners: 'The licence conditions mean what they say and if you ignore them or if for any reason your behaviour on parole gives cause for concern your licence may be revoked.' Once that happens the parolee must surrender himself and return to prison or be subject to arrest as a prisoner unlawfully at large. In certain cases, the Board advises the addition to the licence of extra conditions to suit individual circumstances. For instance, the parolee may be obliged to reside or to work where directed by the supervising officer, or to accept psychiatric treatment, or to keep away from certain specified places or persons. Unlike what happens frequently in America, however, parole licences in England avoid the inclusion of conditions (such as abstaining from drink) which are deemed to be unrealistic or impossible to enforce.

Revocation and recall

The decision to revoke a licence and recall to prison is in principle made by the Board at one of its panel meetings. The supervising officer has to report back to the Home Office, and if the matter is considered sufficiently serious it is referred to the Board. This takes time, and in cases of urgency the Home Secretary can recall first and refer to the Board later for confirmation. If such confirmation is not given the offender must be released again. The recalled offender has no right to a hearing or to an appeal, but he can make written representations to the Board before the final decision is made, and it is customary for a member of the Local Review Committee to interview him and pass on any representations he makes on that occasion.

If a parolee is charged with a further offence, unless he is also in breach of conditions for not reporting or for other reasons, and unless he is thought to be dangerous, the Board has not hitherto taken action to recall, otherwise it might seem to prejudge the finding of the court. Once the court finds the parolee guilty, the Board then orders his recall, unless the matter is considered insufficiently serious to warrant such action. If the parolee is convicted by a higher court, the judge himself can order a revocation of the parole licence, but if he does not, then the Board is free to do so. In theory, the courts should always be told when they are dealing with an accused who is on parole, but in practice they may not always know. Recalled offenders, unless paroled a second time, remain in custody until released in the normal way at the date they would have gone out had they not been granted parole.

Certain categories of prisoners are subject to parole supervision and liability to recall for longer periods. For prisoners under twenty-one when sentenced, or for recidivists given extended sentences, the parole licence lasts to the very end of their sentence. The reason for this provision is that such offenders, even if not paroled, are subject to compulsory supervision during their remission period. Those under sentence of life imprisonment may be released at any time, but the licence, and with it the liability to recall, lasts until death. The supervisory conditions can, however, be altered or relaxed after some years. In practice, life prisoners are rarely released having served less than nine years, although cases are usually first put to the Local Review Committees after about seven years. Release of life prisoners is complicated by the Home Secretary's statutory obligation to obtain the views of the Lord Chief Justice and the trial judge, if the latter is still available. This is normally done, and the views made known to the Parole Board, before they consider a life sentence case.

The selection of parolees

All prisoners sentenced to more than eighteen months are eligible for consideration, but relatively few are chosen. Up to 31 December 1970, 4,140 (that is 20.4%) of a total of 21,404 determinate sentence cases eligible for first review, were recommended to the Home Secretary for parole. The percentage was low when parole first began, only 8.5% of those eligible on 1 April 1968 were recommended. This led to newspaper comments about parole being a cruel hoax, serving only to raise prisoners' hopes unjustifiably. The percentage was higher in 1969 (25.2%) and 1970 (26.1%), but even so the majority are still being refused parole.

In the government White Paper explaining the intentions of parole legislation,[3] (*The Adult Offender*, Command 2852, December 1965) it was proposed that 'release on licence would be limited to those who were likely to respond to generous treatment and who were not regarded as a risk to the public'. The avoidance of risk to the public was emphasised by the Home Secretary, Mr Roy Jenkins, in the course of a House of Commons debate. In reply to a question implying that parole might be used as a means of relieving overcrowding in prison, he explained that overcrowding was affected far more by other matters than parole 'which is likely to affect a fairly limited number'. He added: 'I cannot see a Home Secretary in his right mind taking risks, even for his own interests, of releasing prisoners who might be dangerous when he would be held very directly personally and Parliamentarily responsible . . .'[4]

In a later debate, Mr Jenkins was more explicit in his estimate of the likely proportion of releases. He said: 'In my view the board will be considering about 750 to 1,000 cases a year and not recommending release in all, whereas the total cases eligible in any year would be, in excess of 4,000.'[5]

A release rate of 750 out of 4,000 is 19%, quite close to the actual results. The decision whether or not to release on parole is entirely within the discretion of the Home Secretary and the Parole Board. Nowhere have any precise criteria been laid down. Only very general indications exist of the kinds of facts taken into account in reaching a decision. Clearly, parole recommendations have tended to follow the cautious, highly selective policy which was from the outset the intention of the Home Office.

The first Annual Report of the Parole Board gave an idea of some of the factors taken into account.

> A proper balance between the welfare, rehabilitation and reformation of the prisoner and regard for the protection of the public . . . Particular attention is given to the prisoner's behaviour in custody . . . Indications that deterioration will occur if custody is prolonged are in favour of release . . . His past record – domestic, occupational and social – is a relevant factor. Has he had a settled and stable home life? Has he had a good record of regular employment? Has he been previously convicted, and if so, of what type of offence? . . . Has he previously been under the supervision of a probation officer, and if so what was his response? . . . What was the nature and gravity of the offence? . . . The weight to be attached to these matters varies from case to case . . . Thus the availability of suitable accommodation to receive the prisoner on release is a prerequisite of suitability for parole. A recognised danger of failure . . . lies in the return of a prisoner to the locality and circumstances of his crime or crimes, and in the resumption of former criminal associations.

A more succinct version of considerations in selection was given by Lord Hunt recently in the Ashwell Prison Magazine in answer to questions. He stated: 'Local Review Committees and the Parole Board consider every relevant aspect of the offender's past life and circumstances, the nature and circumstances of his current offence, reports on his response to prison treatment, the latest reports on his home circumstances, work prospects and other questions bearing on the situations which may arise in the event of his early release. It is not possible to single out particular aspects without giving a misleading impression of how a final decision is arrived at. But it can be said that domestic problems may be a factor pointing in favour of parole; absence of religious convictions is not a relevant factor; the type of offence may be a factor against parole, especially in regard to risk to the public or particular individuals.'

The generality of these selection criteria, and the absence of specific rules, leave the authorities free to use the maximum amount of discretion in each individual case. On the other hand, the attempt to bear in mind a multiplicity of vaguely defined indicia, some favourable and others unfavourable to the granting of parole, leads to decisions that are largely subjective, and therefore difficult to justify and liable to unexplained inconsistency. From the prisoner's stand-point, the situation invites distrust, because he sees himself subjected to adverse decisions based upon considerations which he cannot challenge or control. It is also difficult for any independent observer, who wants to form some opinion about the parole system, to understand what is happening. Since it is nowhere laid down what level of reconviction risk is tolerable, what kinds of offences make a prisoner unlikely to deserve parole, or what is the relative importance attached to the contradictory demands of deterrence and rehabilitation, it is impossible to know whether the system is operating a consistent policy. So long as the criteria of suitability for parole remain so vague, it is impossible to say whether the authorities are being unduly strict in refusing three-quarters of eligible candidates. At the opposite extreme, if exact point by point criteria were fixed and publicly announced, freedom to take into account individual circumstances would be curtailed.

2 *Parole in England: some comments on the system at work*

D. J. WEST

Is Parole fulfilling its purpose?

The main assumption underlying parole is that some prisoners, if released at the right time to appropriate guidance and support from probation officers, can be influenced away from further crime. In order to test this proposition, one needs a systematic comparison between similar offenders released with and without parole supervision. As Irvin Waller demonstrates in a later chapter, considerable technical difficulties confront research of this kind, and the results so far obtained suggest that the effect of casework and supervision upon likelihood of reconviction is much less than is generally supposed. Be that as it may, so long as the granting of parole does not actually lead to an increase in crime, it can be justified on both humanitarian and economic grounds. Men in prison are largely idle and unproductive. It costs a lot to keep them closely guarded, and meantime their dependents often have to be supported at public expense. If prisoners can be got out into the community, and encouraged to perform normal social functions, the benefits to their own morale, as well as to their families and to society at large, extend far beyond the statistics of reconviction.

In its Report for 1969 [paragraph 8] the Parole Board noted that recalls of parolees to prison, either for breaches of conditions or for the commission of further offences were infrequent, totalling less than 5 per cent of the number of releases during the year. Unfortunately this statistic, though impressive at first sight, means rather little when one considers the length of time offenders are on parole and at risk of recall. A large number of parolees are under supervision for quite short periods. In the year 1970, for example, over half of those released had parole periods of less than six months, and a quarter less than three months. The Parole Board appears to recognise this as a cause for concern, devoting four paragraphs(63-6) to the topic in its report for 1970.

Such short periods of supervision are obviously unsatisfactory. A parole supervisor cannot seriously be expected to exert much influence upon a prisoner, whether in relation to general social rehabilitation or in trying to prevent reversion to crime, in less than six months. The lengthy and costly process of reviewing cases for parole, and the administrative machinery for providing supervisors, is often invoked for the sake of giving offenders no more than a few extra weeks of liberty. One reason for short parole periods is the way the law has been framed. Since no prisoner can be paroled until he has served a year, offenders sentenced to terms less than two years three months can never be given as much as six months on parole, even if they are released the very first day they become eligible. In practice, owing to the complexities of the review system and the need to arrange for supervision, it is not always possible to release a prisoner promptly as soon as he becomes eligible.

A deliberate policy of caution on the part of the parole authorities also contributes to the number of offenders with only short periods of parole. In the year 1970, a total of 175 offenders with sentences of six years or more were recommended parole. All of these would have been eligible for at least two years on parole, but in fact 48 of them (that is 27.4%) were given less than six months and only 14 (that is 8.0%) were given as much as two years on parole.

The reasons for postponing the parole of some long-term prisoners until just a few months before they have to be discharged anyway has not been fully explained. It looks as if the parole authorities are reluctant to grant more than a minimal period of parole supervision to those offenders who have committed particularly atrocious crimes meriting long imprisonment. If that were so, the policy would be hard to justify, since the gravity of the crime has already been taken into account in fixing the sentence, and ought not to count against the offender a second time. Alternatively, it may be that these very serious offenders are considered such grave risks that the authorities are unwilling to assume responsibility for letting them loose upon the public for very long in advance of the obligatory release date.

This second explanation was the one put forward by Lord Hunt, as chairman of the Parole Board, in the course of a debate in the House of Lords on 17 February 1971.[1] Referring to the relatively few recommendations for release of men serving long-term sentences on the occasion of their first review, Lord Hunt said: 'The main and obvious reason for this has been our concern for the public and the risk which we consider that many of these offenders would represent to the public if they were released at so early a date as at the first third of their sentence.' It would seem, therefore, that the refusal of parole at first review to all but a few long-term prisoners is, in Lord Hunt's opinion, quite justifiable and hence no special problem. He did, however, go on to point out that repeated refusals of parole in long-term cases may involve suffering on the part of prisoners whose hopes are repeatedly raised and dashed. He proposed overcoming this difficulty by abolishing the right of long-term prisoners to an annual review for parole.

The problem of deciding the proper time to grant parole highlights a major anomaly in the English system. Since parole is regarded as a privilege, it tends to be given to the better behaved and less serious offenders. On the other hand, in the interests of society and of the offender, it is the more dangerous and desperate cases who stand in greatest need of supervision on release. As the law now stands, unless granted parole, these offenders are discharged without any supervision whatsoever. A previous Criminal Justice Act (1961) very sensibly provided for compulsory after-care for discharged long-term prisoners, but unfortunately, with the advent of the parole system, this was repealed.

Since the Home Office and the Board have complete discretion in the granting of parole, it lies within their power to deal with this problem. They could give much greater recognition to the need for a substantial period of supervision in long sentence cases. Particularly in the case of abnormal or sexually dangerous criminals, whose style of life needs to be directed away from hazardous situations, a period of parole probably provides more protection to the community in the long run than continued detention followed by release without supervision. For such decisions to be made, the Parole Board needs the backing of a well-informed public capable of tolerating the disasters which must occasionally ensue when serious offenders are paroled. At present, the newspapers and the public show a concern for crimes committed by parolees that is ridiculously at variance with their lack of interest in crimes committed by ex-prisoners who are released without supervision.

In practice, it looks as if the solution to the difficulty of providing for the more serious cases will lie in extending restrictions rather than by more generous parole. In his speech to the Lords on 17 February 1971 Lord Hunt referred to the dilemma faced by the Board when considering prisoners thought to be a continuing risk to the public who would have to be released shortly without any restraint at all unless they are granted some period of parole supervision. His suggested solution was to apply to all long sentence prisoners something like the provisions at present in force for extended sentence cases. That means compulsory supervision following release even though no parole has been granted.

The parole system exists primarily to select the right kind of prisoners for early release; but whether intentionally or not it serves other useful functions in addition. The enlistment of a Parole Board that included some distinguished judges and experts, all of whom took a keen interest in the work, has produced some beneficial side effects. At an early stage Board members found that the information available in prison files was woefully defective, especially in relation to the circumstances of the crime for which sentence had been passed. As C. H. Rolph, himself a former member of the Parole Board, wrote: 'When the parole system started, the "documentation" was awful. Governors of prisons knew almost nothing about their inmates and had grown perplexedly (and sometimes resentfully) accustomed to not knowing.'[2] The needs of the parole system, and requests from the Board, wrought a change for the better in prison files that was long overdue. Since all prisoners potentially eligible for parole were liable to come under the scrutiny of the Board, it became imperative that every file should contain an adequate personal and criminal history. One suspects that the prison authorities learned a great deal more about their clients in the process.

Parole has, without doubt, stimulated a great deal of activity and discussion about prisoners and their needs, both by the public at large, and among those working in the penal services. The Home Office and the Board have held regional conferences with representatives from Local Review Committees in order to discuss their common problems and the grounds on which parole recommendations should be made. Sample cases have been considered by different groups, and then discussed collectively, in an effort to attain consistent standards. In addition, Board members have made numerous visits to individual prisons and discussed the parole system with both officers and inmates. Informal discussions go on all the time with Home Office officials on methods of collecting and recording information, and ways of speeding and improving selection. It may well be partly a consequence of this effort that the percentage of prisoners declining to allow themselves to be considered for parole has decreased.

Suggested improvements

Experience in England has brought to light a number of problems. Some of these might be remedied by changes in practice, others are inherent in the system and could not be changed without legislation. One example of the latter, which has already been mentioned, is the brevity of the periods of parole supervision provided for prisoners with sentences of two years or less. It seems a pity that in drafting the original statute, when fixing a minimum period to be spent in prison, the lawyers did not also fix a minimum period of parole of some six months. That might have caused some offenders with only a short period of custody at stake to decline parole, but such persons would probably not be the type to need or to respond to supervision by a probation officer.

One objection to a minimum of six months of parole for all cases is that some offenders don't really need supervision, and would waste the time of the probation and after-care service. The solution to that, however, is simple. The Home Secretary has power to vary the conditions of a parole licence, and in such cases the Board could recommend that he delete the condition of supervision. Moreover, the probation officers have discretion about the amount of contact necessary for each case.

Another way to ensure an adequate period of supervision for those at present eligible, without discouraging offenders from accepting parole, would be to reduce the time that must be spent in prison before being paroled from a year to six months. An offender with only eighteen months of imprisonment could get up to six months of supervision. A further consequence of this change would be that men sentenced to terms between twelve months and eighteen months would also become eligible, but for lesser periods of parole supervision. It could be argued that since such cases would be generally less serious, lesser periods of supervision would be justified. Such a reform would have the further consequence of bringing into the ambit of parole a larger proportion of the prison population. While in principle this might be considered desirable, it would increase the numbers that would have to be dealt with by the parole selection system and by the parole supervisors.

The parole system has already been strained by a large increase in numbers. This is partly the consequence of more people being sentenced to imprisonment for terms exceeding eighteen months. It has been suggested by some critics that parole may have indirectly contributed to this by causing judges to step up their sentences to counteract the possibility of early release. However, since Lord Parker of Waldington, when Lord Chief Justice, has said that it would be improper to allow parole to influence sentences, one must hope that this is not the explanation. One likely factor in the increase in the prison population is the introduction of suspended sentences, which have been imposed on cases that might previously have been dealt with by a fine or probation. Accordingly, when these offenders are caught again, they tend to go to prison for longer than would have been likely under the old system.

The necessity for all cases to be considered by the central Parole Board before release also creates something of a bottleneck. One effect of the increase in numbers has been a serious overloading of work onto the Parole Board, obliging members to attend panel meetings nearly every week, and to study as many as thirty-five bulky dossiers in preparation for each occasion. Especially for those members who travel from a distance to the meetings in London, this must represent a considerable slice out of their working week, and create difficulty in giving adequate attention to parole cases while keeping abreast of their ordinary duties. A substantial increase in membership of the Board in 1970 went only a small way towards alleviating the situation. A further increase took place in 1971, linked with a scheme for holding panel meetings in the provinces. This may prove to be a satisfactory solution, but of course the larger and more scattered the Board the more difficult it will be to preserve consistency of standards.

One danger of too heavy a case load is that it may leave Board members insufficient time to deal with urgent decisions about cases in which time has not permitted the circulation of preparatory documents. At panel meetings Board members must often reach quick decisions relating to recalls and other matters which they have not been able to consider in advance. It would be unfortunate if such critical matters were to be taken hurriedly. It is understood that the Board is considering how this important duty may be better discharged. The decision whether any particular breach warrants revocation of the parole licence calls for a good deal of discretionary judgement, and a man's liberty, perhaps for a substantial period, depends upon the outcome.

Apart from indefinite increases of Board membership, which must surely reach a point of diminishing returns, the problem of overloading might be solved by giving greater responsibility to Local Review Committees.[3] As it is, a large number of parole decisions concern the release, only a month or two in advance of normal discharge, of rather ordinary offenders against property. These cases do not involve any serious considerations of risk to the public, or any threat to the system of justice. It seems rather wasteful of public money and experts' time to have such cases deliberated by judges, psychiatrists, criminologists and senior probation officers, after they have already been considered and put forward by a Local Review Committee. It would be more than sufficient to have these short-term cases scrutinised by just one or two Board members, or by the officials of the Parole Unit, with a referral to a full panel of the Board only if some cause for doubt emerged.

The English parole selection procedure, with its three stages of scrutiny, takes a long time to reach a final decision, and leaves prisoners in suspense in the meantime. The Home Office guide tells prisoners: 'Normally it will be within three and four months after your interview by a member of the Local Review Committee that you can expect to be told whether or not you are to be paroled . . . In some cases, decisions can take a good deal longer . . .' This period of waiting can be very trying to the prisoner, and if his hopes rise only to be finally dashed by a refusal, for which no reasons are given, his feelings of frustration and disillusionment are understandable. Administrative arrangements can be hurried along, but only up to a point. However well-oiled, the machine must take time to turn over.

Some gain might be had by letting prisoners know at the Local Review stage whether or not they were being recommended for further consideration. Those turned down would realise that they had better reconcile themselves to a further spell in custody, for only in exceptional circumstances could they expect the decision to be reversed. Supplying the prisoner with reasons for refusal is a more difficult problem. Since the decision is so subjective, and influenced by so many factors, precise reasons are difficult to formulate. Moreover, since he can do nothing to alter such considerations as public notoriety, bad record, mental instability, and rejecting family, the prisoner can be both discouraged and wounded if these reasons are quoted. On the whole, and notwithstanding the arguments to the contrary set out by Evelyn Shea in a later chapter, it is probably impracticable to do more than inform prisoners of the range of considerations taken into account in all cases. On the other hand, if the criteria on which the Review Committees and the Board made their selection could be defined more clearly and publicly, that might go some way towards allaying suspicions of injustice.

The initial and most crucial sifting out of parole cases is done by over forty different Local Review Committees. It would be unrealistic to imagine that all of them could operate in the same way and maintain precisely similar standards. Comparability of standards is rendered all the more difficult by the selection procedures, which govern the kind of offenders received at different prisons. A Review Committee at an open prison, for example, will be dealing with the cream of the prison population, none of whom can be considered dangerous, otherwise they would have been kept in closed prisons. In contrast, Review Committees at closed, high security establishments will be dealing with prisoners who have been considered too desperate or too dangerous for ordinary prisons. If the first committee recommended 90% for release, and the second recommended none, they might still be applying similar standards.

The Home Office's own research unit took an interest in this problem of differing standards. First they calculated a statistical expectation of reconviction, based upon such antecedent criteria as age and number and type of previous offences. Then they compared the reconviction expectation of offenders recommended for parole at each prison with the reconviction expectation of the total populations at those prisons. They found that each committee tended to select the better risks from among the population with which they were dealing, but that the degree of risk resulting in rejection varied considerably from one committee to another. It was acknowledged in the Board's Annual Report for 1969 (Appendix 3) that it was in part 'in an effort to remedy the widely different standards which the various Local Review Committees have adopted' that it was decided to refer all low reconviction risk cases to the Board regardless of unfavourable recommendations at local review. Whether this measure eliminates inconsistency entirely one may doubt. A certain amount of idiosyncratic variation is inevitable so long as the system of criminal justice makes use of large numbers of locally recruited lay jurors, magistrates and parole selectors. The obvious alternative, which is decision-making by Home Office officials, or by a professional judicial body, carries the danger of a centralised bureaucracy which might become secretive and over-timid.

The relationship between the authority of the Home Office and that of the Parole Board deserves some comment. One cannot avoid having some sympathy with prisoners who believe that the existence of a Parole Board leaves them still at the mercy of the Prison Department, and unlikely to be granted parole if that Department disapproves. Certainly the prison representative and the reports compiled by prison officers have a powerful influence upon Local Review Committee decisions. At a different level, Parole Board members are fully aware of the attitude of Home Office officials to the release of certain types of offender who are liable to provoke public scandal if anything goes wrong. While it is true that the Home Secretary rarely reverses a Parole Board recommendation, this could be explained if the Board's policy was so cautious that cases likely to be rejected were hardly ever put forward. Influences of this kind might also help to explain the Board's reluctance to give long-term prisoners an adequate period on parole.

In life sentence cases there are more tangible reasons for the suspicion that the Home Office exerts considerable influence. Before ever the Board was set up, Home Office officials had long been accustomed to making decisions about the release of life sentence cases, and had acquired special knowledge of the political, social, ethical and judicial considerations involved. Under the present system, the Home Office still exercises discretion at what stage to refer particular cases to the Parole Board, and when it does refer a case it attaches to the papers its own reasoned recommendations about if or when the prisoner should be released. If release is recommended, a date as far as a year ahead may be suggested to the Board, in order that arrangements can be made for a phased relaxation of custodial restrictions. It is widely believed that, after many years of close confinement, too drastic a transition to freedom can be harmful. Since it takes the Home Office many months to produce its proposals (see *Annual Report for 1969*, paragraph 41) these arrangements have the result that recommendations must be made by the Parole Board for release a year later on the basis of reports written up a year before. Recommendations made under such circumstances cannot be altogether reliable. It would seem that in the consideration of life sentence cases the Board has not achieved quite the same immediate control over the system as it has in ordinary determinate sentence cases. Fortunately the problem is administrative rather than legal, and therefore more readily open to change. It is, however, a problem of increasing importance. The number of persons under sentence of imprisonment for life has increased from 89 at the end of 1955 to about 770 at the end of 1970. Lord Windlesham, during the Lords debate on parole in February 1971, mentioned that since the abolition of capital punishment the number of life sentence prisoners who cannot safely be released is likely to grow. 'Already there are 71 who have served more than 9 years including 17 who have served more than 13 years.'

Finally, the connection between parole policy and sentencing policy must be mentioned. Except in life sentence cases, where the Board and the Home Secretary jointly decide the length of imprisonment, there should be, in theory, no connection between the sentence imposed and the decision to parole an offender when he becomes eligible. The length of imprisonment merited by the offence has already been determined by the sentencing judge, so that the Parole Board is left free to consider each case on its individual merits at the date of eligibility, which is fixed by statute. In practice, however, there is a tendency to deny or delay parole to serious offenders serving long terms of imprisonment, while granting parole more generously to lesser offenders. A continuance of this policy must in the long run increase the differential penalties for serious crime, since long sentences are being reduced little or not at all, while shorter sentences are frequently being reduced by one third. This change in the scale of punishments may not be intended by the Board, or desired by the judges, but it appears to be an inevitable consequence of the way the system is being operated.

In ending up this brief description of parole in England with a few critical comments, no adverse reflection upon the persons responsible for operating the system is intended. Quite the contrary. My own experience as a member of the Board, and the contacts I have enjoyed with Home Office staff, members of Review Committees, and probation officers, have deeply impressed me with the conscientiousness and fairness with which the persons concerned carry out their parole duties. The system itself may have certain drawbacks or obscurities, but it has, by and large, been operated with progressive efficiency and success, in spite of occasional uninformed public criticisms. The credit for this is due in large part to the earnest efforts and varied skills of the Board members, the goodwill of Home Office staff, and the ability of the chairman to inspire the loyal collaboration of colleagues. In the last resort, penal reforms depend as much upon the willingness of people to try to make them succeed, as upon formal statutory provisions.

3 *The Local Review Committee*

J. P. MARTIN

Whatever the details of the structure of a parole system it would seem essential for there to be some sort of local organisation. Irrespective of where the decisions are taken certain parts of the process have to be located where the prisoner is. This applies not only to an interview stage, if there is one, but to the assembly of information – about his present condition, whether he is in contact with his family (if any), whether welfare work is being done on his behalf and so on.

Given that some of the procedure must be locally based the question then is what sort of organisation is needed, and what powers should it have? Although, strictly, this question has two parts the answers are interdependent so that both have to be considered together.

It is an interesting historical point that, whereas the Parole Board is now seen as the key feature of the system, in the original Bill no Board was envisaged but a major part was to be played by a body almost identical with the Local Review Committee. In the Second Reading Debate the Attorney-General (Sir Elwyn Jones) explained that

> The proposed selection procedure is that selection should be based on a continuous process of assessment within the prison organisation . . . Each case will be considered periodically by an informal committee at the prison . . . That informal committee at the prison will consist of the governor, a senior probation officer in the district and a member of the board of visitors or visiting committee approved by the Secretary of State for the purpose. The committee will have all the avail-

> able information about the prisoner, and oral opinion from those in daily contact with him . . .
>
> The committee will be responsible for recommending which prisoners should and which should not be released, the final decision resting with the Secretary of State.[1]

The only difference between this informal committee and the actual Local Review Committee is that an independent member has been added, on the suggestion of Mr T. L. Iremonger MP who argued in Standing Committee that

> there should also be, as one of those sitting in judgment on the proposition that a man should be paroled, A. N. Other. He should be a layman. He should not be involved in the penal process in any way whatsoever. He should not have been involved in the judicial process that led to the man's conviction, or in any judicial process which might follow. He should be absolutely uninvolved. What is more, he should be changed fairly frequently. He should come from outside, be of the outside, and yet he should take part in these proceedings.[2]

Although there were arguments in parliament about who should take the final decisions, it seems to have been agreed that the function of a local committee was essentially to screen those eligible for parole. Apart from adding the independent member, the conception of the local committee as such was virtually unchallenged during the passage of the Bill. Now that the Act has been in operation for some years it is possible to reconsider some of these points. Comments are made on general considerations and should not be taken to be based on the experience of the LRC of which the author is a member.

Membership of the Local Review Committee

First of all, how appropriate is the structure of the LRC for the task it has been assigned? It seems that the present structure derives from two assumptions: (*a*) that the granting of parole is a part of the administration of penal treatment, and (*b*) that involving, as it may, important decisions about the liberty of the subject, considerations of justice and of public confidence in the system demand the participation of people independent of the administration. Both arguments were expressed at various stages during the passage of the Bill. It is, of course, possible to rely on either assumption in planning a parole system: for example, American systems tend to emphasise an independent review body, while the Scandinavian countries see it as a matter of administration. The various emphases may well relate to the significance of the period of parole in affecting the length of the offender's stay in custody. Generally speaking, the longer the potential period in custody the more likely the system is to adopt a quasi judicial approach with at least some emphasis on questions of due process. Not surprisingly the British system is a compromise.

Is it, however, an effective compromise? Are the various interests represented in the most suitable way? The role of Governor in an English prison is so crucial for the running of the Institution that the system might not be taken seriously if he were not involved. Furthermore, it is probably a very good thing that Governors, who are necessarily much concerned with what happens inside their institutions, should be reminded that the ultimate test of the system is provided by the post-release performance of those who have been through it. If the prison administration is to be involved in the system at all then representation at governor level is essential.

The argument in the case of the Probation and After-Care Service is somewhat different. Ideally, as Mr Iremonger suggested, the person who ought to be involved should be 'if possible, the probation officer who will be responsible for him on licence'.[3] In practice this suggestion has been taken to be impossible, and the service is represented by *a* Senior Probation Officer. He or she will, therefore, bring professional expertise to the committee, but will not usually represent the views of the potential supervisor. Yet the point that his or her views should be considered is a good one. It is, after all, usually the practice in the officer's probation work both for his views to be sought, and for his unwillingness to take on a particular client to be respected. Surely in professional terms there is no reason why parole cases – which may be particularly difficult to handle – should be treated any differently?

If this view is accepted the problem becomes an administrative one, of how the potential supervisor learns enough about a man to decide whether or not he can help him, and of how this view is taken into account in making the parole decision.

Even now it is sometimes possible for potential supervisors to meet their clients before deciding whether or not to try to help them, and so initiating their relationship before the parole decision is taken. This is roughly analogous to the pre-sentence investigations of probation officers. It is, however, time-consuming, and can only be done for a proportion of cases. The officer will have to balance the value of such work against time spent on, say, home enquiries, contacting potential landladies, employers and so on. Whatever the form of such preliminary work its results may be crucial to parole prospects and should somehow be communicated to the LRC.

At present the potential supervisor's view is only likely to be represented to the LRC if the Welfare Officer has been in contact with him. This may happen as a matter of routine,[4] but will otherwise depend on whether the prisoner himself has raised problems with the Welfare Officer. It is outside the scope of this essay to discuss how far potential supervisors should be free to refuse to assist particular individuals, but knowledge of their view of a man's situation would surely be of value to LRCs in making their recommendations.

All this points to the significance of the Prison Welfare Officer in the deliberations of the LRC. The Parole Board summarises this part of his work as 'the task of co-ordinating information from social work sources which will help assess the man and his environment, and lastly he supplies the Local Review Committee with an essential report'.[5] This is irreproachable as far as it goes, but does it go far enough? What part should the Prison Welfare Officer play in the deliberations of the committee and, indeed, should he be a member of the committee?

The possibilities range from a role analogous to that of the Probation Officer's relationship to his Court to being a full member in the same way as the Governor. Some members of parliament, such as Mr Iremonger, appeared to think the Welfare Officer should be a full member of the committee, but in the main the question was ignored. It might be argued that the matter is not important because the Welfare Officer's views are invariably expressed in a report – which may include a recommendation – on the Parole Form LB2 which includes all comments made by the prison staff. The right to express views, therefore, is not in question. These views, moreover, will reach the Parole Board if the case is considered by the Board.

The real issue is the right to influence the LRC's discussions and, if necessary, to make the dissenting recommendation which any member of the committee may write. The main argument in favour of membership is the simple one that the Welfare Officer is the person who, in most cases, is best informed about the applicant and his circumstances. He, or she, therefore is potentially the best judge of the applicant's prospects. He is, furthermore, experienced in dealing with prisoners' problems and may well be able to make a more realistic assessment than anyone else on the committee. His effectiveness as a member ought, therefore, to be particularly high.

The contrary arguments might be that, as someone actually working with the prisoner, the Welfare Officer might be too 'close' to the situation to make a balanced judgment, and that if prisoners knew that he was a member of the LRC he might be exposed to some pressure to reveal the committee's recommendations. By itself the argument of closeness is not particularly strong: close acquaintance with prisoners is not usually conducive to facile optimism, and is not regarded as an objection in other branches of the penal system, such as Borstal, where analogous decisions have to be made.

The argument about 'security' of information implies not only that the Welfare Officer should not be a member of the committee, but should never know the committee's recommendation. This boils down to the question of whether members of the Probation and After-Care Service are to be regarded as responsible professional people. If not, they should not be in the job.

In the long run, moreover, it will be the Welfare Officer's job to interpret the parole decision to the prisoner and to encourage him to use it in as therapeutic a way as possible. This can only be done efficiently if the Welfare Officer knows how the LRC reasoned in particular cases. If, therefore, parole is to be used as anything more than a legal device for letting some prisoners out early without too much risk to the community, the rationale of the system must be understood among prisoners, and this implies the full involvement of the Prison Welfare Officer.

Underlying these specific points is the more general issue of whether the parole decision is to be seen primarily as a judicial or as a treatment decision. If the judicial element is emphasised it could be argued that the important thing is to make the decision which best balances the expectation of rehabilitation against the risk to the public, and that provided this is done carefully the only requirement is to communicate the decision to the prisoner concerned. This would be to take a more limited view even than is taken of sentencing decisions – which are frequently intended to have some influence on the attitudes of those outside the courtroom.

A therapeutic approach, on the other hand, clearly implies that the decision-making process should be used as an influence on the attitudes of the individual concerned and, so far as possible, on the whole group of men eligible for parole. This requires that those involved in treatment should be responsible for decisions, subject to some check on matters of major public importance. In the last resort nothing is so salutary for therapists as to be confronted with the consequences of what they do, and it is an unfortunate feature of the judicial and penal systems that this rarely happens. Anything that will strengthen the involvement of institutions with the outside world is surely to be welcomed.

On all these points, in my view, the balance of advantages lies with involving the Prison Welfare Officer as a member of the Local Review Committee.

The involvement of members of Boards of Visitors or Visiting Magistrates in Local Review Committees has never seriously been questioned and requires little discussion. Such members, although associated with the prison administration, have a degree of independence often combined with experience as lay magistrates. As such they form a group of informed laymen who can relatively easily be brought into the parole system.

The position of the independent member is somewhat more doubtful. In Parliament, at least, the idea was put forward by Mr Iremonger in the passage quoted above (see p. 33). He saw this independent member as the Chairman of the LRC, thus emphasising to the prisoner that he was being, in effect, judged by a judge unconnected with the former proceedings or with the prison administration. In this way the prisoner would see he was getting a fair deal. (Mr Iremonger's proposal involved the prisoner appearing before the committee.) Such a scheme has obvious attractions but on examination one is led to wonder how valid they are.

The first of these is that to a prisoner *anyone* who has authority to come into a prison and take part in such proceedings is likely to be viewed as part of the administration – one of 'them'. Outsiders can become accepted by prisoners, but this always involves a process of 'testing' and takes a long time. In any case the fact that the prisoner does not appear before the LRC and probably does not know who the members are, leave alone who is in the Chair, reduces the potency of the argument that the independent member's presence will be seen to ensure impartiality.

The second, and more important difficulty, relates to the independent member's very inexperience of the penal system. He, or she, will probably have no experience of Courts, Probation Officers or Prisons and may well be at a disadvantage when in a committee all the other members of which are more or less involved in the system. At the very least he or she can, if determined enough, see that cases are not dealt with in a cursory manner, and can be a watchdog on the principle of 'equality of consideration'. The making of assessments, however, is more difficult. Paradoxically much will depend on how experienced the independent member can become. The more experienced he is the more effective he is likely to be in making assessments and expressing his independence. The independent member, then, should probably attend a larger number of meetings than the other members; this is possible when the LRC is divided into panels so that its members do not sit more than three or four times a year.

This, however, raises the general question of the desirability of continuity in the membership of the committe. Local Review Committees tend to be fairly large, so that the work load on individual members can be reduced by dividing the committee into panels. This means in practice that an outside member may not sit more than a few times a year, while the Governor or his Deputy, and probably the Welfare Officer, may attend far more frequently. The obvious advantage of this system is that people with jobs outside do not suffer too much disruption in their work and are so able to find time to sit on the committee. The disadvantages may be that some members become much more experienced than others, potentially gaining more influence, and variations in standards may develop between the panels. The second of these may be counteracted by the vigilance of the Home Office and the Parole Board, but the former can only be solved by finding members who are prepared to sit more often. This might be more easily achieved if they were asked to sit, say, on a monthly basis for six months and then not at all for the rest of the year.

Procedure

Documentation The dossiers provided for members of Local Review Committees have a relatively standard list of contents. They tend to be rather voluminous, and some members of LRCs find it essential to make a brief summary of certain items. The biggest weakness of the system is that much of the information is inevitably out of date. There may, for example, be a copy of the Probation Officer's report to the sentencing court, but little or nothing to indicate how far the home situation has changed. If the committee is lucky the Welfare Officer may have been in touch with the home area for some reason or other and in such cases there will be more up-to-date information to go on.

Details of the offence are usually rather limited, and reports of the trial, Judge's remarks and so on are virtually non-existent. This is no bad thing. Local Review Committees are better suited to considering the prisoner as he is, and what his prospects may be, than trying to weigh up the more legal considerations, particularly where the LRC is only dealing with one out of a number of accomplices.

The interview The interview is probably the trickiest part of the LRC procedure. *The Local Review Committee Rules 1967*[6] require that any prisoner, willing to be interviewed, shall be interviewed by a member of the LRC other than the Governor of the prison (or presumably anyone deputising for him). This means that the interviewer may be either a professional social worker (a probation officer), or a Magistrate or a lay member of the Board of Visitors or an entirely independent person. The obvious problem is to ensure that such varied interviewers manage to conduct equally good interviews.

Some LRCs appear to have tried to solve the problem by delegating 'the task of interviewing prisoners solely to their probation officer members'.[7] With all due respect to the undoubted merits of probation officers this would seem to indicate undue modesty on the part of the other members. Certainly the risk of one type of bias might be reduced, but another might be amplified. This is because a previous failure to respond to probation is a fairly frequent feature of the careers of prisoners eligible for parole, and it might be that some prisoners at least would regard a probation officer interviewer with some suspicion. They might feel that they were back on the same track as before instead of being given a chance of a fresh start. This in itself might be evidence of an unpromising attitude since parole, if granted, would involve co-operation with a probation officer. On balance we know so little about the merits of particular classes of interviewers that it is probably wise to leave the matter open until more definite information is available.

Indeed, in the last analysis there is no evidence at all on how satisfactory the interviews are. In the early stages of the scheme it became clear that, as the Parole Board put it, 'certain interviewers have considered it part of their function to make an assessment of the applicant's suitability for parole'.[8] This was a misunderstanding both of the Rules and of the Home Office notes for Local Review Committees. The Board has made it clear both in its Reports and at the conferences held for members of Local Review Committees that the purpose of the interview is 'to assist the prisoner to put his own case for being granted parole and to elucidate the particular points which the prisoner wishes taken into account; and the advice issued to all prisoners eligible for parole also explains this and contains an assurance that the interview is not an assessment.'[9]

The conduct of the interview is crucial in establishing the prisoner's confidence in the system, for the simple reason that it is the only part which he personally experiences. Some scepticism may remain even if the interview is well conducted, but if it is not the prisoner can have little basis for faith in the whole operation. How can confidence best be engendered?

As no survey of LRC interviews has been conducted I can only indicate points which have occurred in my experience, without claiming that one person's practice is anything more than a single example.

Obviously the prisoner should be made to feel as much at ease as possible; this may be helped by introducing oneself, being generally polite and pleasant and, above all, unhurried. For the interviewer the interview may be one of a series to be completed in a morning, but for the prisoner it is his only chance of expressing himself face to face with a member of the LRC. It is useful to be familiar with the prisoner's dossier, but it is as well to keep this knowledge a bit in the background so that the prisoner feels he is able to tell his own story; the interviewer can, however, raise points which the prisoner may have overlooked.

It is important to stress that this is the prisoner's chance to put his own case, and that the interviewer's sole concern is to help him to do so. This is the spirit of the Rules and of the Home Office notes for guidance. It is also as well to indicate that the interviewer is only one out of several members of the committee and that, in any case the actual decisions are taken by the Home Office and the Parole Board; the local committee only makes recommendations. Strictly speaking this is true, but it must be recognised that a negative recommendation almost has the force of a refusal as, in most cases, the parole unit refuses parole on the strength of the recommendation. Indeed the official notice to the prisoner in such cases states that the Secretary of State 'does not feel justified in referring your case to the Parole Board'. In this way one can reduce the risk of raising false hopes which a prisoner might have if he thought the interview had gone well.

From reading the dossier the experienced LRC member may have a shrewd idea of the likely outcome of the application, but this must be firmly ignored in order to avoid giving the prisoner the impression his case is already decided, or that he is being judged during the interview.

Some prisoners may know fairly clearly what they want to say, and may indeed already have submitted a written application; with them the interview is relatively easy. The main need is to be sure that the prisoner has not omitted anything important. The problem of elucidating any prisoner's case is a delicate one. On the one hand the LRC member knows the kind of points the committee is likely to take into consideration – and he should see the prisoner addresses himself to the important issues. On the other hand he should not so prompt the prisoner as to produce an interview record which implies that the prisoner has a greater degree of self-awareness than is in fact the case.

It is fairly safe to preface the interview by saying that the LRC will probably be most anxious to learn of anything that will suggest that the prisoner has a good chance of settling down and keeping out of crime if he is granted parole. If necessary he can be prompted on the most obvious points such as whether he has a home to go to, any job prospects, friends who will help him – anything in short which suggests he is now more likely to settle down than in the past.

Sometimes prisoners bring documents which may be intended to help their case. Two important classes consist of letters from potential employers, and from voluntary associates or others wishing to help the prisoner on release. Obviously these must be studied, and their existence noted in the report of the interview. Normally copies will have been included in the file but it is important that they should not be overlooked. Such papers present the LRC with problems of interpretation. (This may even literally be the case as, for example, when a prisoner produces a letter written in, say, Greek, purporting to be an offer of employment as a waiter in a restaurant.) In most cases it is unlikely that the LRC will know much, or indeed anything, about the writer or his relationship with the prisoner so that it will be hard to judge the reality of the situation. Sometimes there may be supporting evidence, such as visits by the associate to the prisoner, but in its absence the LRC can do little more than draw the Parole Board's attention to the possibilities and hope that a social enquiry report will reveal the significance of the relationship.

Greater difficulties arise over the treatment of potentially bad points. Suppose a man's relationships with his family are poor and they don't really want to have him back, or that previously he committed further offences while on probation. Situations of both these types may weigh heavily against the prisoner; should the interviewer draw attention to them? If the prisoner does not realise how important they are his views on them may simply go by default, while if he has to be reminded of them this fact in itself says something about his awareness of his own problems. There does not seem to be a clear-cut answer. My own feeling is that it is fairest to put these points to the prisoner if he is clearly going to ignore them, but to inform the LRC that it was necessary to do so.

Finally, when the interview is over, how is the prisoner to be given confidence that his case will be truly and well represented? Again there is no infallible rule, but my own practice has been to begin the interview with a preliminary discussion to see which points were to be made, then write a brief note on each *in consultation with the prisoner.* At the end I either show it to him or read it aloud and ask him in roughly the following words 'Is this what you want to say, and is there anything else you think should be added?' Only after he is satisfied is the interview concluded.

The difficulty, however, remains that the interviewer cannot help forming some judgement of the person he has seen for, say, twenty minutes, and this will nowhere be written down but almost certainly used in the discussion. The Parole Board itself recognised 'that it is inevitable that impressions will be formed at the interview which will be discussed at Local Review Committee meetings, at which the interviewing member should be present, but at the same time it must be remembered that the purpose of the interview is to convey the personal representations of the prisoner'.[10] The whole procedure involves the interviewer in a somewhat ambiguous exercise in role-playing: first he is the prisoner's spokesman, second he is a man reacting to another man, and finally he is one of a small group of people who make a recommendation on the case. As interviewer he may well be the most influential member of the panel, having recently had a face to face encounter with the prisoner. It may say something for the conscientiousness of interviewers that this combination of the roles of advocate and member of the panel has been the subject of so little comment.

It could well be argued that the alternatives might be worse. If the prisoner saw no member of the panel he could well feel that the whole process was arbitrary and impersonal, while an interview with a group of people might run the risk of turning into something rather like a trial.

The meeting of the Local Review Committee panel

The meeting of the panel normally takes place about a week

after the interview, and a typed copy of the interview report is included in the papers relating to each applicant. All the members of the committee should therefore have read all the papers relating to each man being considered. The numbers considered by any one panel may vary, but in an afternoon a reasonable figure would seem to be about a dozen. Some can be decided quite quickly, others, particularly where there is supplementary information from the Welfare Officer, may involve considerable discussion.

One of the best features of the system is that the members of the panel do not have to agree, but may submit dissenting reports. Indeed the panel may be equally divided in some cases. Discussion, therefore, does not have to be exhaustive; differences of opinion are not surprising in a situation where judgement has to weigh limited information and assess the imponderables of character and motivation. There are no statistics on how often panels are divided in their recommendations, but it would seem to happen in only a small minority of cases.

The possibility of divided recommendations also makes the choice of chairman of the Local Review Committee somewhat less important. Practice evidently differs: 'some Committees have elected their prison governor as chairman, others, whether at the request of the governor himself or as a matter of principle, have not done so'.[11] As governors are likely to attend more panel meetings than other members there might perhaps be less of an impression of prison domination if one of the other members chaired panel meetings and this certainly happens in some LRCs.

The chairmanship of the Local Review Committee as a whole, which may only meet as such annually, is less important than the question of chairing panel meetings.

Perhaps the most interesting procedural points concern the contributions respectively of the individual 'case officers' and of the Welfare Officer. In some prisons there is a system of designating officers as 'case officers' having special responsibility for a group of prisoners on whom they prepare regular reports. They are probably the officers with the best knowledge of individual prisoners. Practices vary, but some LRCs invite any such officers who wish, to attend the panel meeting to give their views on the response of prisoners to their period of imprisonment. This does not mean that they are present when decisions are taken. Usually consideration of a case opens with a discussion of their report, and continues after the officer has withdrawn. Such personal impressions may be of great value in illuminating the question of whether a man's attitude in prison has taken a more constructive turn. This involvement of officers may also have beneficial effects in encouraging the staff to take a more personal interest in inmates, and to think about the long-term aims of imprisonment. At the moment the participation of case officers appears to be voluntary, but it is to be hoped that it may grow.

The extent to which Prison Welfare Officers should be involved has already been discussed in this chapter, so that here we need only mention that at present, even though not a member of the committee, the Welfare Officer is frequently in a position to play a major role in the discussion of the panel. He, or she is usually the member of the staff best informed about the social circumstances of the prisoner. He is likely to have seen the prisoner and discussed his prospects with him, and may well have been in contact with social agencies in the home area. He is often able to give a verbal report on the latest stage in any casework that has been going on. In short, his role is crucial.

The greatest strength of the LRC is that it can call on people who are in close contact with the prisoner; its greatest weakness is probably that it may have to make recommendations on the basis of inadequate information about situations outside the prison. The Parole Board has rightly stressed the need for LRCs to receive both Police and Social Enquiry Reports,[12] and arrangements have been made to make Police Reports available when requested. Prison Welfare Officers on their own initiative may obtain social enquiry reports and where this is done it is most helpful.[13] In both cases the difficulty arises if the panel decides it needs further information but no procedure for adjourning the meeting has been devised. It may be that some LRCs have experimented with this, but there is no mention of it in the first two reports of the Parole Board.

The tenor of the discussion in the Board's 1969 *Report* suggests that LRC decisions need to be based on better information. The administrative problem remains of how to provide this in a reasonably economical way. A substantial proportion of cases can be decided on the basis of the information available at present, and it would waste valuable police and probation officer time to collect new reports from them. Others require up-to-date reports and a decision cannot properly be made without them. What is needed is a means of screening cases so that the appropriate reports can be obtained before the LRC has to make its recommendations.

Several alternative solutions can be imagined:

1. The committee might delegate one of its members to read the papers as long before the meeting as possible – say three weeks – having the power to request any reports thought desirable. This would have the disadvantage that it would precede the interview and would therefore be unable to take into account any points raised by the prisoner in his application. It would have the further disadvantage that the remainder of the committee might disagree with their colleague's judgement so that there could still be a residue of cases needing reports at the time of the panel meeting.
2. The committee could make conditional recommendations to the Parole Board. For example they could recommend Parole subject to a 'satisfactory' social enquiry report. This device has certainly been used on some occasions under the present procedure. It suffers from the disadvantage that the Parole Board may not know quite what the LRC was concerned about as the panel's reasoning may not have been fully expressed in its recommendation. It also leads to delay in that the request for information will not be made until the parole unit of the Home Office has had time to read the papers and find out what is required.
3. A more satisfactory solution might be the one suggested earlier in this chapter in relation to the problem of continuity and consistency between panels. This would be that panels would sit regularly over a period of six months, so that where necessary cases could simply be adjourned to the next meeting, reports being obtained in the meantime. At the end of the six-month period there would have to be an extra meeting to consider cases on which reports had been requested. This procedure would have the additional advantage of improving the consistency of judgement. In some cases there would be delay, but this need be no greater, and would probably be less

than, the delay which would occur if the parole unit had to request information.

4. A variant of (3) would be for the committee to make a provisional decision delegating the final one to the Chairman who would make it in the light of the reports when they were available. This would have its disadvantages, particularly if the panel was on the verge of producing divided recommendations.

My own preference would be for having panels sit regularly for six months and then have six months off. This would have advantages in terms of continuity and obtaining of reports, while the burden should not be excessive.

The second main problem facing the LRC is the relative weight to be attached to information about the prisoner's behaviour in prison compared with that referring to his life outside. The danger here is that too much weight may be attached to behaviour in prison, particularly if it is bad. The importance of bad behaviour in prison is stressed by the Parole Board in its *Report* for 1969:

> Those who have offended seriously against prison discipline do not inspire confidence in their ability to keep out of trouble on discharge. Moreover, to recommend the more troublesome characters for parole would have the effect of undermining discipline in the prisons, and possibly lowering the morale of better-behaved prisoners who had been refused parole on other grounds.[14]

No doubt in time the facts on this question will be revealed by the Home Office research into Parole, but for the present a word of caution should be uttered. In the somewhat analogous situation of Borstal, Mannheim and Wilkins found that paying attention to behaviour in the institution led to relatively inaccurate predictions.[15] The prison situation may be different, but the 'halo' effects of good (or bad) behaviour on the opinions of prison staffs should not be underrated. The man who resents his imprisonment, and shows it, may well be highly motivated to get parole and keep out of trouble; he may nevertheless get a name for being unco-operative. In general, predictions about behaviour outside an institution, made an the basis of behaviour within its artificial world are probably best viewed with scepticism. Very little information is available to prison staffs as to the after history of ex-inmates, so that in many cases they have no feedback about their predictions, while their direct knowledge is of the man under stress in abnormal circumstances.

Really serious offenders may be a different matter, but it can be argued that they will be punished by the proper authorities (Boards of Visitors, Visiting Committees or even the Courts) and that the Parole Board should avoid appearing to augment the penalties imposed. Much will depend on the circumstances of such offences, the subsequent behaviour of the men concerned and their implications for parole.

One must also raise some doubt concerning the Parole Board's emphasis on the value of Police reports to Local Review Committees. As at present constituted, with infrequent panel meetings, LRCs may not always have enough experience to assess the seriousness of crimes and this particular function might be better left to the Parole Board which has some hope of establishing a national standard. What would be of most value at the LRC stage would be a police assessment of the offender's degree of involvement in criminal society, as this has been shown to have a direct bearing on the chances of failure on parole.[16]

A police report adequate for the purposes of the LRC could probably be made available with little extra effort by simply expanding the report normally made by the police to the prison governor at the time of the offence.

Problems at the prison level

A number of more general problems remain, which we must now discuss.

The first concerns the difficulty of assessing when a man is 'ready' for parole. When the parole scheme was originally proposed, the White Paper on *The Adult Offender*[17] argued that a man's response to imprisonment reached a peak, which was the point at which he would have the maximum chance of success if released. Part of the idea of the parole scheme was to allow for the occasions when this 'peak' occurred before the normal date of release. This argument may have derived from the far more flexible Borstal system, but the parole system as developed lacks the sensitivity required for this purpose. For one thing the peak could only be taken into account if it was reached between one-third and two-thirds of the duration of the sentence (with a minimum of 12 months) and, in most cases, only if it was near the parole eligibility date. As cases are usually only reviewed on the anniversary of the parole eligibility date the man who reaches his 'peak' mid-way between two reviews is unlikely to be released within several months of the 'peak'.

The difficulty is that no one really knows how to identify the 'peak', if indeed such a phenomenon actually exists. What the LRC has to do in practice is to try to assess whether the man's attitude is 'promising' at the time of the review. This may be more realistic, but it does rather undermine the notion of a precise relationship between parole and treatment.

A second difficulty which sometimes confronts the LRC is presented by the man whose problems seem so great that he might well fail on parole unless his passage to freedom was made by gradual steps. The LRC tends to be faced by the need to make a decision between 'parole' and 'not parole' when what is required is something in between. This problem was particularly acute in the early days of the scheme, but one gets the impression that, through the work of welfare and after-care officers, hostel vacanies are being earmarked so that the LRC may recommend parole subject to the prisoner entering a certain hostel. The Parole Board has fully accepted the spirit of such recommendations and, in its 1969 Report commented that 'In a number of cases it has only been possible to recommend parole because an "After-Care Hostel" or "Half-Way House" has been prepared to accept the prisoner at the time of his release.'[18]

Prison hostels and out-working schemes have also been used in a rather similar way to meet the same problem, and this again has been a result of fruitful contacts between members of LRC and the Parole Board.[19]

A more awkward choice has occasionally arisen when men eligible for parole have at the same time come to the top of the waiting list for the special psychiatric prison at Grendon. Refusal of parole might not be a very auspicious beginning of a period of treatment so the LRC will be concerned as to the right thing to do. A possible compromise has been to recommend an early review – usually in six months – so that the decision can be taken in the light of progress at Grendon.

The third area of difficulty – perhaps as yet insufficiently recognised – is the problem of men whose potential period on parole is relatively long – say two or three years. This implies that their original sentences would have been six or nine years for, presumably, rather serious offences. The same point holds for men with Life sentences. It is, simply, that many members of LRCs find it difficult to contemplate a man being granted the full period of parole possible under the legislation. It is impossible to know exactly what this belief is founded on. It may be the seriousness of the original offence, the potential dangerousness of the prisoner, or even a belief that the period under supervision should not be excessively long. The Parole Board has commented on this issue as follows:

> The Board has the difficult task, especially in more serious cases, of balancing the dangers of early release against the risks of detaining an offender until he has to be released without statutory supervision. Some serious and potentially dangerous offenders, who are rightly refused parole at first review, may be considered more favourably at subsequent reviews, when a relatively short period on licence may seem justified for the sake of establishing supervision and control on release and providing help in the process of resettlement.[20]

As the LRC can rely on the care with which the Parole Board considers the question of public safety, it has perhaps to be on its guard to remember that Parliament really did intend prisoners to have a genuine chance of release after one-third of their sentence.

Long sentences raise the embarrassing practical problem of how to conduct parole interviews with men for whom the issue is crucial. Such men are often model prisoners and inevitably all their hopes are pinned on the review procedure. The interviewer has to walk an unusually precarious tightrope between raising false hopes on the one hand, and deepening cynical despair on the other. The problem is almost bound to be aggravated with the passage of time as the process of keeping men's cases under review implies something like annual interviews. For prisoners with little hope of release in the near future such a procedure, even though intended to ensure they are not forgotten, may be cruelly tantalising. No doubt the whole procedure will be refined as experience of Lifers increases, but for the moment they represent a particularly delicate and taxing problem for members of Local Review Committees.

These, then, are the major problems that confront LRCs. In the last resort they are essentially matters of judgement, of balancing quite different sets of considerations against each other – the seriousness of the offence, the risk of further crime, the chances of settling down, repercussions on the morale of other prisoners and, indeed, on prison discipline. The LRC, therefore, has to be seen as a Parole Board in microcosm, doing a similar job but with a rather different emphasis. All its strengths derive from being a local body concerned with a limited number of individuals – men whom its members have met, and with a share in the life of the same prison community. Inevitably the LRC has to focus on the behaviour and prospects of the individual. It should be prepared to back its judgement of prisoners as people and leave the major issues of public policy to the Parole Board.

How well do Local Review Committees do their job?

At the present state of knowledge it seems impossible to assess how well LRCs do their job. In the first place there are no criteria of success. The Parole Board has explicitly stated that LRCs should not think they have made wrong decisions if their recommendations are reversed by the Board. This is because the Board may have more complete information, and may be concerned about consistency in the treatment of accomplices who may be considered by several LRCs.[21]

The only cases where it is reasonably certain that a correct decision has been made are those where parole has been successful; where it has been refused no one can be sure that it might not have been successful. As almost all negative recommendations by LRCs go no further than the Home Office all that can be said about such cases is that no risks were taken.

Clearly there have been considerable differences in the proportion of positive recommendations made by various LRCs. If we assume that all cases considered by the Parole Board were positively recommended by LRCs (which may be a very slight over estimate) we can see from the figures in the 1969 *Report* that in the South-East Region alone the proportion of eligible cases considered by the Board averaged 35%, but ranged from 20% from Wandsworth to 73% from Springhill. The Springhill figures were possibly affected by the very small number involved, but are almost certainly explained by the selection of inmates to be found in an Open prison. Wandsworth, on the other hand, is a prison with many serious recidivists so that it is not likely to be a good recruiting ground for parolees.

It is difficult to say much about the variation in standards between LRCs. The only statistically correct way of doing so involves the use of prediction scores. This has been done by the Home Office Research Unit, with the result that

> it has been possible to show that Local Review Committees create their own standards for selection and that the Parole Board broadly accepts these different standards.[22]

It was as a result of this analysis that the procedure was revised so that cases were forwarded to the Parole Board on the basis of their prediction scores even when rejected by the LRCs. This has been done on a quite considerable scale:

> Additional cases are being forwarded to the Board at the rate of 700 per year in an effort to remedy the widely different standards which the various Local Review Committees have adopted.[23]

If we bear in mind the fact that 2,576 cases were considered by the Board in 1969, it would seem that the true rate of positive recommendations by LRCs in England and Wales might, therefore, have been of the order of 1,875 out of 6,788 (28%) compared with an apparent average of 38 per cent.

The Board itself appeared to have some preference for following LRC recommendations in such cases:

> Whereas some of the cases were, as was anticipated, marginally suitable for parole, in the majority the reasons for rejection by Review Committees were clear, and the Board was in full agreement. Experience in considering some of these cases has confirmed that although they come within the group where the risk of recurrence is slight the nature of the risk in

> the individual case may be such that it cannot be tolerated. The particular circumstances of an individual case may suggest to the Board a greater risk than the reconviction expectancy calculated from a necessarily limited range of items.[24]

This tends to reinforce the view that in most cases a negative LRC recommendation has almost the power of a veto. The evident disparity in standards between LRCs therefore has the disturbing implication that a prisoner's chances of parole may to some extent be influenced by the procedure of allocating him to a particular institution.

Short of having a monolithic system some discrepancies between local decision-taking bodies are inevitable. The variations should, however, be kept under review and reduced as far as possible. The first National Conference between the Parole Board and representatives of LRCs in fact decided 'to give priority in the programme of visits (by the Board) to those prisons whose Review Committees appeared to be most at variance with the Board in their recommendations for parole.'[25] The difficulty of ensuring reasonable comparability between committees is part and parcel of the more general problem of LRCs that they have so little feedback about the results of their recommendations. It may, indeed, be a more serious difficulty than the lack of up-to-date information about home circumstances (which is gradually being remedied). The Parole Board is ready to inform LRCs of its decisions in particular cases, but it is clear that little use has been made of this opportunity. There might be scope for an occasional dialogue between members (or a member) of the Board and a Local Review Committee concerning its work, but this could only be done on any scale if the necessary statistics were regularly available. Such a procedure should, perhaps, be reserved for LRCs whose recommendations showed some consistent difference from the average, which was linked with unsatisfactory results.

Various possibilities of feedback can be envisaged. Perhaps the most valuable would be to do for an LRC what has been arranged at some of the Conferences for LRC members, namely to receive reports on the post-release history of specific men, so that the committee can see how its judgement worked out in practice.

Any such comparison could only relate to men actually granted parole but but there is probably a need to see if men refused parole subsequently made good and what lessons could be learned from their experience. If this were not done one suspects that it might become too easy to think of mistakes in granting parole to men who were reconvicted, but to ignore those other mistakes which kept men in prison unnecessarily.

If parole is ever to have a reasonably scientific basis – and this should stand far more chance of being achieved than scientific sentencing – studies of this kind are essential. Unfortunately it is difficult to envisage much being arranged at LRC level simply because there are many LRCs and such 'feed-back' exercises are time-consuming and difficult to arrange.

This brings us to the difficulty of devising any 'training' for LRC members. In the absence of the definite information which should become available when the Home Office research on parole is published it seems unlikely that any better method of training will be devised than the periodic Parole Board – LRC conferences with their mock panel meetings and account of what actually happened to individual parolees. It might be possible for an individual LRC to conduct a post mortem on a sample of its cases, but the time, effort, and expertise involved make it improbable that such an operation could be completed in more than a handful of prisons. The publication of the Home Office research results, therefore, remains likely to be the most important single influence on the work both of the Board and of Local Review Committees.

The future of Local Review Committees

It is safe to say that Local Review Committees have a future. Quite apart from their positive merits, the Parole Board could not operate without the screening of cases which LRCs undertake. More than sixty per cent of cases in 1969 were excluded from further consideration on the advice of LRCs. Even if the Parole Board was substantially augmented so that it could just cope with the numbers, it would still be essential to have an operation at the prison which involved the prisoner and those with direct knowledge of his circumstances.

This may become increasingly important if the trend towards

emphasising due process of law becomes more important in our society. While the granting of parole is seen primarily in therapeutic terms it may be possible for the system to continue to operate in the present somewhat informal way. Should the system ever be assailed from a legalistic angle, however, it is difficult to imagine that decisions involving the liberty of the subject could continue to be taken without prisoners having the right to know, and question or comment upon, all information considered by the Board. Such a development would not necessarily be to the advantage of prisoners as it might well lead to a more routine and rule-bound operation. It might also, in order to make the questioning of information possible, have the effect of shifting the balance of the procedure to a local level.

The Parole Board concluded its 1969 Report by speculating whether its load might be reduced either by some delegation to LRCs or by a regionalisation of the Board.[26] In the event the regional solution has been tried first, but one would hope that some delegation to LRCs has not been permanently ruled out.

It can hardly be argued that local committees should decide on major cases. As has been explained in this chapter the committee's perspective is inevitably more parochial than that of the Board, and this militates against giving it substantial powers of decision. With lesser cases, however, perfectly adequate decisions might well be taken by LRCs. The correlation between their recommendations and those of the Board is already high, and the tenor of the Board's Reports suggests that disagreements are more frequent in major cases. In minor cases, where the period of parole involved is no more than a few months, no substantial risks would seem to be run. Indeed the alternatives to be balanced would be the risks of release, say, three months early but under the supervision of a probation officer as against unsupervised release three months later. This sort of choice would seem to be quite within the competence of the LRC provided it is supplied with adequate information about home circumstances.

Such delegation would have considerable administrative advantages. Almost all the necessary documentation is already done at the LRC stage, and obtaining social enquiry reports could easily be arranged by prison welfare officers even if in the larger prisons this meant that some augmentation of their numbers might be necessary. Three considerable savings would be achieved: (*a*) the Parole Board's time. A high powered body would not have to spend much of its time dealing with minor cases. (*b*) Waiting time – at present an LRC's decision is reached roughly within a month of opening the dossier, and within a week of the interview. It is uncommon for the decision of the Parole Unit or the Parole Board to be reached in less than a further two months, thus increasing the anxiety of the waiting prisoner. (*c*) Administrative costs. There is no information about the time spent by members of the parole unit per case, but referral to the Board must incur substantial costs in photocopying alone.[27] Obviously this is essential for cases referred to the Board, but if the number could be reduced the savings might be considerable.

What disadvantages might there be? Some LRCs might tend to depart rather far from the average. This might perhaps be checked by statistical scrutiny by the Home Office parole unit with the possibility of referring occasional cases to the Parole Board. This might be done in any case when members of the LRC disagreed.

Possibly the major difficulty might be that prisoners might seek to bring pressure on the prison members of the LRC if they knew that decisions were taken locally. This risk, however, exists already in the case of negative decisions. If necessary it could, perhaps, be guarded against by adding another non-prison member to the committee, but in view of the Borstal precedent such a measure might not be needed.

Finally we should mention the complex problems of giving reasons for refusal of parole. The bureaucratic reason for not giving reasons is an old one – if reasons are not given they cannot be questioned, nor can they be misinterpreted. Given the frequency with which prisoners petition the Home Office on various matters it is easy to understand that no one wants to open the floodgates of petitions against refusal to grant parole. The whole process might do nothing more than build up bad feeling and a constant toing and froing of arguments and recriminations.

Yet across the interview table how often does the interviewer feel that the application will be refused but that the man needs insight about the reasons if any change of attitude is to be achieved. It must never be forgotten that among the sticks and carrots of the penal system the possibility of parole ranks as the largest carrot. The tragedy of the system is that no one has yet solved the problem of using such a powerful incentive in a therapeutic way.

At present Welfare Officers may give discreet hints about reasons – if they know them – but the lack of any sort of individual treatment programme and the understandable concern for security in serious cases, mean that the most powerful lever in the system is barely used. If the penal system is to get beyond containment and into the business of trying to change attitudes, some way must be found of using the parole system in a more constructive way. In this operation the Local Review Committee could well move beyond its present role of being a sieve, albeit an effective one, for the Parole Board.

4 *Caring for offenders on parole*

W. H. PEARCE

What happens to a prisoner when he is released from one of our prisons? He gets out early in the morning, he will stand up in his own clothes or, if they were too bad, he will have been provided with alternatives at the clothing inspection. Financially the man will have the savings he has accrued during his prison stay which, with present earnings averaging a few shillings per week, are not going to amount to much. He is likely to have, if this is inadequate, a sum from public funds equivalent to the first payment he would otherwise receive from the Ministry of Social Security. In addition he will have a railway warrant to his home. His employment cards, however, are almost certainly going to give the game away to prospective employers that he has been in prison.

What are the advantages to a prisoner of release under parole supervision? The United Nations Congress on the Prevention of Crime and the Treatment of Offenders held in London in 1960 defined the purpose of after-care as 'to bring about the reintegration of the offender into the life of a free community and to give him moral and material aid'. The developments since that time have been forward looking in theory, even if something of a credibility gap has developed between theory and practice.

When the system works smoothly, the offender released on parole reports to a local probation officer who is already apprised of his circumstances and anticipating his arrival. This officer has a dual responsibility, to advise and befriend the ex-prisoner, and at the same time to exercise a degree of surveillance with a view to forestalling breaches of licence or the commission of further offences. He wields the sanction of referral back to the Home

Office and the Parole Board should the ex-prisoner prove unco-operative, but in the great majority of cases this issue does not arise. The probation officer's prime concern is with the rehabilitation of his client.

It can quickly be established that the efficiency or otherwise of after-care depends in part on the ability to help offenders with work and provide them with various material physical resources. However, too much emphasis must not be placed on this aspect. There is no doubt that prisoners themselves during their sentence place a high importance on the ability of their probation officer to find them work. From the security of their cells they indulge in a great deal of employment day-dreaming. The result is that prisoners on release have unrealistic expectations and are bound to be disappointed with what they actually achieve. Work conditions in many prisons, with short hours and constant interruptions, do not equip men for the demands they meet outside. Probation officers, therefore, must not measure success on parole solely by success in employment, although a man's attitudes and efforts in this regard can be a useful test. Of course, it is clearly essential for the probation officer to be familiar with employment opportunities in the locality, and if possible to have a register of employers likely to be sympathetic. He also needs to establish good contact with the Ministry of Labour. Firm work commitments are perhaps best made immediately following release, but it needs to be remembered that the real barrier to employment is not a man's criminal record – but his skill.

As regards financial support, the same caution applies. It would be preferable for all prisoners to be released in possession of savings accrued as a result of their own conscious, deliberate and rewarded work and achievements during imprisonment. In many prisons this does not happen, but the English prisoner can at least rely on aid from the Ministry of Social Security once he has a settled address. For the homeless this may prove more difficult, but consideration will be given later to the use of half-way hostels to meet this problem. In addition, it is important for the probation officer to have small sums of money readily available for emergencies, so that he can, for example, compensate members of the community who have helped the Service by providing accommodation for ex-prisoners. Indeed, the provision of a 24 hour emergency service as part of the after-care facilities is probably worthy of consideration.

Probation officers try to help offenders to integrate with legitimate social groups, but this task is made difficult by the nature of the prison system, which tends to reinforce the barriers between prisoner and community. There is also the danger that imprisonment may have weakened ties with wives, families and friends. Interestingly enough, however, American studies suggest kinship ties may in fact sometimes be strengthened. Rifts between parents and son or husband and wife may be healed by the trauma of the sentence – although conflicts may reappear on release. There is one easy means of alleviating the problem of separation. Letters and visits represent the prisoner's only contact with the community and are of great importance to his well-being and future resettlement. It would be a considerable improvement if restrictions on letters were minimal and family visits to the prisoner were to be positively encouraged by the authorities.

A number of other factors concerned with the prisoner himself must be taken into account before going on to consider the part the community may play. It is a common experience that, as the date of release approaches, the prisoner's attitudes and feelings become more constructive and positive. Although this phenomenon has been noticed by many people, prisoners are rarely picked up at this stage and given appropriate support when the opportunity presents. It is a reasonable hypothesis that the greater the contact the offender has with the community during sentence, the more likely he is not to offend again. The serious problem in terms of reconviction lies with the homeless client who has no roots and no family ties. Focus placed on providing these seems to be the *raison d'être* for hostels. Conversely, a man who has close family ties and goes back to them may in fact be going back to that very environment which caused his delinquency. Even so, such an environment prima facie would seem more desirable than homelessness, and anyway should lend itself to community focused treatment. One might justifiably make further speculations in this area, namely that if the prisoner's family background is fairly stable he represents a better risk. In other words, a history of marital upset in the past is an area the probation officer must reasonably explore. He must also encourage his parolee not to associate with other ex-offenders and if possible to steer him towards new friends.

For all these requirements it goes without saying that the probation officer must be fully aware of the needs of his client and the effects, results and implications of his recent prison experience. Contact should have been made whilst the man was still in prison and, in collaboration with the prison welfare department, the probation officer should understand the total diagnostic and treatment situation before release on parole.

As regards the involvement of the community with paroled prisoners, it is probably valuable to restate the philosophy behind this concept. One basic assumption is that the community has a responsibility for the rehabilitation of offenders. Let one say immediately, however, that where volunteers have been used, or organisations persuaded to participate in after-care programmes, the result has frequently been an increase, rather than a decrease in the work of the probation staff. Nevertheless, it may be true that in some respects volunteers may be able to relate to an offender better than a professional worker. It is therefore important that social workers do not develop any negative exclusiveness about their own skill, so that they disregard the advantages of using well motivated members of the community in this work.

The methods involving the community are limitless, but one of the most important is the voluntary associate schemes, where probation and after-care departments have recruited individuals who will respond to the challenge of helping the ex-prisoner. The volunteers can be people whose interest lies in a number of different areas, some might want to do active personal case work, others may prefer more simple tasks such as babysitting, finding employment or accommodation and other essentially practical functions. It is not possible to categorise precisely the role of these volunteers, their varied performance is best guided simply by the needs of the client. The majority of probation areas in the country have tried to adopt this method, and the degree of involvement in such schemes is one of the most encouraging features in the English penal system at the moment.

It would seem at first glance that the qualities required of a voluntary worker exclude the use of the ex-offender in this work. However, it is quite clear from a consideration of other criteria, that such a person could play a very important role in this area. I am reminded of a phrase in a book by Paul Vere, who wrote, 'Notice that it is not sufficient to bring the delinquent into contact with an individual who can demonstrate *desired behaviour*. We must bring him into contact with an individual who can demonstrate the desired *behaviour change*.' A further reminder of the validity of this concept is ex-President Johnson's comments concerning the idea of involving victims in their own rescue when he said that you do not win a war against poverty unless you involve the poor in a war against it. In England some mental hospitals have exploited this idea, notably the Henderson Hospital, where the patients interpret each others' emotional problems. Within the delinquency field, the principle has so far been applied, with some success, to particular minority problems such as alcoholism, drug addiction and gambling.

Before leaving this subject I would like to differentiate between the role of the volunteer and the probation officer, in case there has been any confusion as a result of my comments. Both use the on-going relationship as a focus to help the ex-prisoner, but thereafter the probation officer acts as the professional, and restricts his performance within the fairly strict conditions and criteria of the formal relationship. He is trained to assess clients' needs and to achieve the desired modification by a regulated use of a relationship. Heavy work loads and many other demands on his time also ensure that he does not become too involved. For the volunteer there are no such restrictions. His relationship is personal, he has more time to give, he need not be so inhibited by his role and he is not invested with the same source of authority as the probation officer.

Ex-prisoners without homes undoubtedly constitute a particularly difficult problem in terms of their re-integration into the community. A number of men and women released on parole are now being accommodated in 'after-care' hostels or 'half-way houses'. If it is understood what these residential establishments can achieve, it becomes possible to recognise the kind of ex-prisoner they can help. They can provide protection for the institutionalised and inadequate offender who has forgotten, or never learned, how to cope on his own. For such a man it can provide a settling which enables him to solve his problems one at a time, giving him continued support at the same time. In this type of shelter, such a man can ease himself into demands of living that most of us take for granted, buying food, making money last, choosing appropriately. Because his ability to form and sustain relationships is impaired, such a man needs companionship, and a hostel can provide him with this. Not only does it provide a community group, but also a peer-group among which he finds others, in various stages of development, who are meeting or have met successfully the problems he is himself facing. It allows him time to adjust until he is ready for independence.

Mention should be made of the prisoner's dependents who, during his period of imprisonment, may in some respects be worse off than the man himself. The majority of dependents will be in need of support and help and the probation and after-care service is now playing a significant role in helping these families. It is now becoming general practice for all prisoners to be interviewed by a probation officer at the time of sentence to ascertain the needs of the family. The family is visited and, if necessary, contact is maintained during the sentence, provided the family agrees. This, incidentally, is an area of work in which voluntary workers can be most effective. The forming of Prisoners' Wives Groups has also proved to be a worthwhile venture, and a recent survey indicates that if they are properly organised they can meet some of the needs of lonely wives, and at the same time play a significant part in re-integrating the ex-offender into society. It is one of the hopeful assumptions underlying 'after-care' that work with the family whilst the prisoner is serving his sentence will build up his confidence in the Service's ability to help, and so cause him to co-operate when released. It is recognised that many of the prisoners with whom the probation officer will have to work have had serious confrontations with authority and are already suspicious or hostile. One of the ways in which it is possible to assist is by showing the prisoner, whilst he is serving his sentence, the caring aspect of authority. In this way the caring and the limit-setting, which is the essence of authority, can be brought together and interpreted to those who are involved; the prisoner, his family and the community.

The need to provide adequate support and guidance for persons who are released from our penal establishments is a matter which has been given considerable publicity during recent years.

The Report of the Working Party on Supervision and After-Care of Persons released from Prisons and Borstals in England summed up after-care in the following words: 'Supervision and after-care is not merely a matter of finding employment and of giving material aid but "casework" concerned with the whole personality of the individual in his social environment.' For this task it is essential that there should be adequate numbers of professional social workers who are trained to understand the motivations underlying human behaviour in the light of psychological theories of human development. The knowledge and understanding of motivation and relationships is of particular value to the professional worker in managing his relationship with the offender in such a way as to earn, and retain, both respect and goodwill. Whilst he must be warmly responsive to the prisoner's real needs, he must be quick to recognise attempts to deceive or exploit him. In other words he needs 'compassionate feeling but dispassionate thinking'.

Despite the progress which has been made in this field, there is still much to be done before those who are involved in this work can feel satisfied with the service they have to offer to the ex-prisoner on behalf of the community. Essentially, there is a need for closer co-operation between those responsible for training in prison, and those who undertake after-care, both before and after release on parole. If this can be achieved, then it would be possible to regard the process of rehabilitation as starting from the date of reception into prison and continuing until the termination of the period of after-care supervision. The success of our penal training methods cannot be assessed by the behaviour or progress of an offender whilst he is serving his sentence – the supreme test is his re-assimilation into society.

The majority of persons granted release on parole have responded to supervision satisfactorily, but inevitably there have been some failures. Parole policy has not restricted releases entirely to 'easy' cases; some of those granted parole have been sophisticated criminals, and others have been convicted of offences of violence. The recall procedures described in the first chapter, which provide for immediate action in cases of urgency, have proved both necessary and effective.

Some of the problems which confront probation officers in their dealings with paroled offenders are revealed in a survey by

Martin Davies (Martin Davies, 'The first parolees', *Probation 16*, 4-10, 1970.) of the Home Office Research Unit. He studied the outcome of 343 offenders released in April 1968. These first releases represented a smaller proportion of eligible cases, and hence probably a more cautiously selected group, than in subsequent parole practice, when the system had got under way and was being operated more confidently. Nevertheless, even in this early group, 28% had been serving sentences of imprisonment for violent offences. Nearly a third of the offenders had little support from their families on release. Most of these unfortunates were either single men, or separated from their wives. In their first contacts with supervising officers, 6% had shown no signs of friendliness, and 12% had been unwilling to discuss their problems.

By 1969, 23 of these early releases had 'failed', either by committing further offences while on licence or by being reported for a breach of parole conditions. Factors which significantly distinguished these 'failures' from the rest included being unmarried, being under 30 years of age, and mixing mainly with criminals.

Although the small percentage of 'failures' is a statistic which may be due to the careful selection of offenders for parole, I believe the efforts of probation officers have also made some contribution. I think this view likely to be confirmed when the Research Unit of the Home Office has sufficient data to compare the reconvictions of paroled offenders with their expected reconviction rates, based upon data collected before parole came into operation.

5 *Parole philosophy in England and America*

EVELYN SHEA

Principal differences

One useful way of learning about prevailing expert opinion on some aspect of the law is to look at model legislation. In this essay we contrast the structure of the English parole system with the provisions and underlying legal philosophy of the 'ideal' system embodied in the Model Penal Code. This Code was published by the American Law Institute in 1962 after some years of study and preparation. The parole structure proposed in the MPC has not so far been adopted by any jurisdiction: indeed, some features of it contrast strongly with those of existing systems. But the Code can be regarded as an authoritative statement of a substantial body of legal opinion in the United States.

At a superficial scrutiny of the English parole legislation in the Criminal Justice Act, 1967 (s.59 to 64) and the American Model Penal Code (MPC, s305.1-205.19) one gets the impression of looking at two entirely different systems. There is first and most obvious a substantial difference in the length of the legislation. Whereas the English statute contains all that is considered important in four sections, the parole provisions of the MPC need nineteen. Why this difference? Does it mean that the English legislation is incomplete? Or that the MPC reverts to the old Prussian tradition of trying to solve every conceivable case by an excessively minute legislation? If we look more closely at what has been considered worthwhile embodying in statutory form, we find the Model Penal Code is not just a more detailed version of the English Criminal Justice Act of 1967, the two differ considerably in content. What is apparently a core issue in one piece of legislation is often treated as a matter of secondary importance in the other, and vice versa. For instance, more than a third of the English parole provisions are concerned with the problem of who shall be competent to decide on parole matters, whereas the MPC deals with the question in one single section (s.402.2). In contrast, the CJA 1967 makes hardly any reference to the central topic of the American legislation: to set up precise guidelines to direct the Board's decisions. The only plausible explanation we can find to account for these discrepancies is that they represent distinctly different views on the purpose of statutory regulations.

England, if we may use such gross a generalisation, still seems to live in the tradition that the election of honest and capable men is the best guarantee citizens can have that the decisions made by their judicial or administrative bodies will be just and appropriate. This is not to say that the English are unaware of human imperfections. But rather than limiting the discretion of its organs by statutory regulations, and thus perhaps interfering with the flexibility of the decision, they prefer to set up a second or even a third body to control the decisions of the first. Hence, the main legislative effort for parole has been spent in creating a hierarchy of parole authorities and in regulating their respective competency, whereas no attempt has been made to formulate any criteria to guide the actual parole decisions. The only other aspect which has been regulated to some extent is that of the requirements for eligibility for consideration.

The American Law Institute's views on the aims of legislation are quite different. The authors of the MPC do not seem to share the confidence of the English in the ability and fairmindedness of their judges and administrators. Neither do they consider the introduction of controlling organs an effective and efficient way of reaching apposite decisions, especially if these bodies are only qualified by an assumedly greater expertise but equally act on a basis of free discretion. They do not, however, take the extreme view that the objective impartiality of the law should entirely replace human discretion, but they believe that 'the law should provide the basic criteria that should guide correctional administration.'[1] They also hold that uniform, predictable standards are over all a better guarantee for just decisions than blanket discretion, even if the price paid is a certain lack of flexibility. One of their major concerns has therefore been to formulate the basic criteria for parole decisions and to set the limits of legitimate state interference. This greater awareness of human imperfection also explains to some extent the noticeable tendency of the American model to try to eliminate meticulously every possible source of misinterpretation. No less than five sections, for example, are devoted solely to the question of reductions or forfeiture of reductions for good behaviour (s.305.1-5).

It is inevitable that a code which attempts to limit the discretion of correctional administration as far as feasible, and to leave no unclear situation, would need more space than legislation which contents itself with providing a frame within which the parole authorities can operate freely. It is not altogether easy to decide which of the two methods is to be preferred. Undoubtedly, the more freedom a truly expert body has in reaching its decisions the greater its possibilities to find an adequate solution for each individual case. On the other hand, really expert bodies are an ideal quite rarely found, and one may well ask whether in view of the inevitability of human shortcomings, the more realistic approach of the MPC is not better suited to protect the individuals concerned, especially as the code only tries to limit, not to eliminate, discretion.

Differing views on the aims of legislation account for a good part of the divergences between the two statutes. The second main factor, which has caused two distinct conceptions of parole systems to develop, can be seen in the difference between English and American attitudes towards the aims and limits of correctional measures. England shares with most European countries a rather ambiguous attitude as far as the aims of punishment are concerned. While reform and rehabilitation are advocated as goals of equal standing with retribution and deterrence, none the less in practice considerable reluctance is shown to use reformative measures in any but innocuous cases. Parole yes, but not for everyone. It is granted only to those offenders whose early release runs little risk of minimising the gravity of their offence, endangering society or reducing the deterrent effect of the punishment on potential criminals. Parole therefore is by no means a measure a prisoner has a right to expect; it is a favour granted only to deserving cases.

In the approach of the American Law Institute retribution and general deterrence still play a part, but the emphasis is on correction. Once an offender is apprehended it is considered the right and the duty of the state to correct this fallen member of society – one feels almost tempted to say at all cost. This means for parole that it is no longer considered as an act of grace but as an effective means of treatment which has to be granted to every eligible candidate. It also implies that the principle – still very much alive in England – of a just proportion between the length of correctional treatment and the gravity of the offence becomes secondary. In England, the length of the sentence is generally assumed to be in a fair proportion to the offender's culpability, and the legitimate duration of correctional measures is strictly limited to this period. In most American legislation, as also in the MPC, these limits have been substantially modified for the sake of efficiency.[2] The actual period of incarceration can extend beyond the period which would have been considered appropriate under a determinate sentencing law. With indeterminate sentences that may vary between specified upper and lower limits, even the maximum term, though it already exceeds what might be justified by the gravity of the individual offence, does not necessarily bring an end to correctional surveillance, but merely sets the limits to lawful imprisonments. This means that according to the intentions of the American Law Institute the parole period can extend up to five years beyond the maximum sentence – a consequence absolutely unthinkable in an English frame of reference. The absolute limit for any form of compulsory correction in Great Britain is fixed by the expiration of the judge's sentence, and neither the parole period nor the recall time can extend beyond this point. The current English law deems it already improper to extend the parole period for ordinary prisoners beyond the date they would have been released had they not been granted parole, i.e. by good behaviour after serving two-thirds of their sentence.

While the MPC, on the one hand, has moved away from the recognition of a just sentence tariff as setting absolute limits for punishment, it tries on the other hand to compensate for the potentially greater loss of liberty by creating special protections against unjustified board decisions. First, it goes far beyond the British practice in providing the prisoner with essential rights, such as, for example, the right to advise with his counsel before both selection and recall hearings. Secondly, as we have already mentioned, it attempts to set up clear criteria to guide the board's decisions. In both respects the English legislation compares very poorly. Safeguards against misguided decisions are not lacking entirely but they are inadequate. For instance, a parolee is not even given the elementary right to a hearing prior to a recall decision. This lack of concern with protection of the parolee's interests has been defended by the argument that for the duration of his sentence a prisoner forgoes any claim to freedom. He has no right to be paroled, or to stay on parole, and hence needs no special protections against unfair decisions. But there is a strong point against such legalistic logic: it endangers the core purpose of parole, which is to prevent the offender from committing further offences. The aims of rehabilitation are incompatible with arbitrary decisions. Offenders should be granted parole whenever by this means the chance of reconviction can be reduced, and they should not be burdened with unrealistic conditions nor recalled without proper cause. This is not to say that decisions reached by the English parole authorities show any of these deficiencies. On the contrary, the English system, as we will see, works in practice surprisingly well. But the potential danger of misguided decisions against which there is no remedy cannot be denied. If for no other reason, the needs of rehabilitation certainly would have justified better safeguards.

THE EFFECT OF THE BASIC DIFFERENCES BETWEEN THE TWO LEGISLATIONS

The process of selection

1. The selecting bodies The choice of bodies to make decisions could not be more typical of the basic approach of the two pieces of legislation. The MPC allocates full power to select offenders for parole to one organ, the Parole Board (s.402.2), but checks this power by carefully restricting its discretion. The CJA 1967, on the other hand, allows almost unlimited discretion, but relies on a complicated filter-and-control system whereby each parole release is liable to scrutiny at four levels, the Local Review Committee, the Parole Unit of the Home Office, the Parole Board and the Home Secretary. The respective functions of these authorities have been described in the first chapter.[3]

The Local Review Committees, which consider all cases as they near their eligibility date, are left to apply their own criteria at their own discretion. The notes of guidance provided by the Home Office suggest a number of considerations in selection, but these instructions have no binding effect, any more than the criteria used by the Parole Board.

The Parole Unit is the only other body which checks every case under review, but now that it no longer seeks to filter out unsuitable cases, its functions are administrative rather than advisory. Nevertheless, it cannot fail to exert some influence on parole decisions. For instance, it can put to the Board additional information which may not have been available to the Local Review Committee, and it has the task of identifying cases which the Home Secretary might wish to veto.

The Parole Board may be regarded as the most important of the selecting bodies, in that it takes the lead in policy, and its negative decisions are final. The membership of the Board, which is voluntary and part-time, includes experts from different fields, each of whom is expected to contribute his special knowledge to a fair solution of all requests for parole. In most American parole boards, the members often work on a full-time basis and do not usually have the special qualifications required for the English Board.[4]

The Home Secretary is the Minister responsible to Parliament for the running of the penal system. In England, parole is a portion of the sentence which is converted by an administrative act, so it is arguable that the Home Secretary, as head of the penal administration, should have the last word on the parole decision. However, he is only given power to veto positive recommendations (presumably those he thinks against the public interest); he cannot parole against the will of the Board. We do not consider this restriction either logical or desirable. It implies that the only kind of error of concern to the Home Secretary is the granting of parole to undeserving cases. The equally possible danger that over-cautious boards deny parole where it would have been appropriate has obviously been neglected. If it was considered proper to give the Secretary of State a right to override Board decisions this power should also have been made to apply to both positive and negative decisions.

2. *Eligibility* (*a*) *The candidate* Both legislations show the same tendency to keep the range of eligible candidates as open as possible. There are no restrictions as to the nature or gravity of the offence. The only requirement is a minimum length of the sentence.[5]

One may question whether the time restrictions in both legislations are really desirable. There is no obvious correlation between the length of the sentence and the need of a period of supervision and help after release. Ideally one should wish to see parole extended to all cases which could profit by a period of supervision, but one has to be realistic about the actual facilities available. Supervising officers are already over-burdened, and one can understand that the legislators were reluctant to ask them to take on the large number of short-term prisoners. Since the danger of deterioration during imprisonment is not so great when sentences are under one year, it follows that if a selection has to be made, the long-term prisoners should be preferred.

(*b*) *The time of eligibility* Fortunately both the CJA 1967 and the MPC have avoided the mistake of several continental jurisdictions, which allow parole only after the offender has served three-quarters or more of his sentence. In England, every adult prisoner sentenced to a fixed term of imprisonment can be released on parole after having served at least one-third of his sentence or 12 months whichever is longer (s.60 [1]). For the American MPC, every prisoner sentenced to an indefinite term of imprisonment becomes eligible upon completion of his minimum term less reduction for good behaviour, or if there is no minimum term, at any time (s.305.6). English prisoners serving an indeterminate life sentence can theoretically be released at any time, although notice must be taken of judges' recommendations as to length of time to be served.

The two pieces of legislation differ not so much in fixing the minimum term for eligibility but in deciding on whether there should be a maximum term after which release on parole becomes mandatory. The English attitude, which considers parole still as a privilege, naturally does not take to the idea of introducing a mandatory release on licence for every prisoner. If the prisoner is not considered worthy of parole he simply has to serve his full term in prison and is then released unconditionally. The authors of the MPC, on the other hand, argue that the longer a prisoner is held in prison because he is considered a bad risk the more he is in need of supervision. Accordingly every prisoner who has completed his maximum term less good time should not be released unconditionally but on parole. Thus, high-risk cases can be held in prison for a considerable length of time and yet still be given a period of supervised freedom.[6] It is certainly desirable to find a means of granting parole to bad risks without thereby unduly endangering the community. One wonders, however, whether the method chosen by the MPC does not solve the problem entirely at the prisoner's expense. It would seem to sacrifice the principle of just deserts for the purposes of correction to a degree unacceptable to a democratic society.

3. *Selection criteria* Professor Wechsler pointed out at the 33rd Annual Meeting of the American Law Institute[7] that there are three possible ways of formulating the selection criteria. These are:

first, to consider release as normal and ask what reasons should be given for denying release;
secondly, to consider retention as normal and ask what reasons should be given for awarding release;
thirdly, merely to state considerations that the board should take into account.

The American Law Institute has opted for a combination of the first and third possibility. Thus, every prisoner should be paroled at the earliest possible date. His release can only be deferred for one of the following four reasons, namely that:

(*a*) there is substantial risk that he will not conform to the conditions of parole; or
(*b*) his release at that time would depreciate the seriousness of his crime or promote disrespect for law; or
(*c*) his release would have a substantially adverse effect on institutional discipline; or

(*d*) his continued correctional treatment, medical care or vocational or other training in the institution will substantially enhance his capacity to lead a law-abiding life when released at a later date. (s.305.9[1])

In order to assist the board in reaching a decision the MPC lists 13 factors that should be taken into account (for instance, the prisoner's personality, his previous record, conduct in the institution etc.). (s.305.9[2]).

It is not an easy undertaking to spell out such criteria, above all the reasons for postponing release. The American Law Institute obviously had to make allowances for the interests of the prison administrations and public sentiment (s.305.9 [1 *b,c*]). Also, the criteria have to be general enough to allow for flexibility, and this inevitably curtails their ability to confine the board's discretion. Yet, even if the criteria arrived at are not entirely satisfactory, they are still useful. Their merit lies not so much in their effectiveness in limiting the board's discretion as in making the members aware of the factors considered essential by the present legislation. Hence it is hoped that the number of decisions based on irrelevant motives will be reduced. In other words, a broad margin of discretion is inevitable in decisions aiming at the individualisation of the sentence. But by formulating clear guidelines, the legislators can at least ensure that the board's judgment is based on rational criteria rather than on half-conscious motives.

One could wish that the English legislature had been more willing to spell out the criteria of selection. The CJA, as well as the Parliamentary debates on the Parole Bill, keep absolutely silent about the basis on which parole should be granted or denied. A further possible source of information, the White Paper *The Adult Offender* which was published in 1965, is not much more helpful. It restricts itself to very general indications such as: 'Release on licence would be limited to those who were likely to respond to generous treatment and who were not regarded as a risk to the public' (para. 4), or, 'that a prisoner's date of release should be largely dependent upon his response to training and his likely behaviour on release' (para. 4).

Some more practical comments can be found in Lord Stonham's Parliamentary address on the parole legislation.[8] He lists several factors, such as antecedents, conduct in prison, prospects after release etc, which in the view of his government should be taken into consideration when reaching a decision. Apart from these few guidelines the English practice is completely free.

It is certainly not up to us to argue against the reserve with which the English Parliament has made use of its legislative powers – it may well be that the election of capable men actually is a better way to secure appropriate decisions than legal rules, however carefully formulated. But one wonders whether, in view of the complicated system of selection, there does not arise an exceptional situation under which a clear statutory regulation plainly deserves preference. Even if we count the Home Secretary and the Parole Unit as one, we are still left with three bodies which decide on the granting or denial of parole. Without concrete legal guidelines, the danger cannot be overlooked that all three will develop their own criteria which, though probably not differing in principle, will certainly put different emphases on different points. Two unfortunate consequences are likely to arise from this: first, the use of inconsistent criteria for assessing cases, and hence a lack of justice, secondly, a general feeling of distrust in each body regarding the appropriateness of the criteria used by the two others. The latter risk can be lessened by good communications. The situation has already been improved since occasional seminars have been introduced where members of the LRCs are given the opportunity of considering model cases and discussing selection criteria with members of the Parole Board. We may add that the abolition of any pre-selection by the Parole Unit, and the introduction of a routine re-examination of all low risk cases, has also lessened the difficulty.

4. *The rights of the parolee* Whether it is considered an administrative act or a quasi-judicial one, the parole decision is of great personal importance to a prisoner. Both pieces of legislation agree that it should not be made without granting the candidate a few essential rights, at least the right to some kind of hearing.
(*a*) *The right to a fair hearing* The CJA 1967 and the MPC explicitly grant each eligible prisoner the right to a parole interview (CJA 1967, s.59 [6*b*], LRC Rules, 3/4; MPC s.305.6/ 305.7), but the right is not granted in the same way or to the same extent in both legislations.

The MPC provides for a hearing either before the entire board or before a member or members designated by the board (s.305.6). The candidate is entitled to 'advise with any persons whose assistance he reasonably desires including his own legal counsel in preparing for a hearing before the Board of Parole'. (s.305.7 [2]).[9]

The English legislation on the other hand does not grant an oral hearing at top level but only before one member of the LRC.[10] A report of this interview is added to the parole dossier (CJA 1967, s.59[5]; LRC Rules, 3). The prisoner has, in addition, the right to make written representations which have to be considered by the Board (CJA 1967, s.59[5]; LRC Rules, 4). No provisions have been made for the candidate to advise with his counsel or any other persons except the prison staff. Still, it may be said that the provisions made by the CJA 1967 are adequate. There is usually no need for a hearing before the Board as the aim of such an interview in England, unlike in the U.S.A., is not to help the Board members assess the candidate through an immediate personal impression but 'to assist the prisoner to put his own case for being granted parole and to elucidate the particular points which the prisoner wishes taken into account.'[11] It is therefore only reasonable that a member of the LRC, as the preselecting body, should perform this task, and certainly it would be less convenient to have the Board travel from London to the various prisons. The right of a parolee to consult his counsel does not seem to us essential for a fair hearing in this context, as there is no need for a person with special legal skills to help a prisoner to formulate his arguments. The parole decision is basically an adjustment of the sentence and, as with the initial sentencing process, it is relatively unburdened with legal questions. As essential as lawyers are whenever the question of guilt or innocence is concerned (for instance in a recall decision), for the parole decision itself any intelligent person of goodwill should be capable of helping the prisoner present his case. One would hope that these qualifications were met by any member of the LRCs. Neither legislation makes any provision for giving the candidate access to the information on which the decision will be based. This is surprising, particularly in the case of the MPC. The right to a fair hearing is not exhausted by merely giving the party concerned an opportunity to state his case before a competent body. In itself, this does not give him adequate protection as long as he does not know on which information his case actually will be judged, and thus has no opportunity to correct possible errors and to adjust his defence. The principle that the knowledge of the evidence is an essential part of any fair hearing, even for administrative decisions, is otherwise firmly established in both legal systems.[12] One would therefore expect that the candidate be given at least a summary of the pertinent information about matters since his conviction – he will already have had access to the documents relevant to his trial. It might be objected that this could cause difficulties for the prison staff if the prison report has been unfavourable. It also cannot be denied that the knowledge of the content of social enquiry reports could in some cases do the prisoner more harm than good. None the less, in our estimation these fears, legitimate as they are, cannot outweigh the interest of the candidates to know on what basis the parole decision is reached.

(*b*) *The right to an explanation for a refusal* The prisoner's right to an explanation if he is denied parole belongs to the same category as his right to be given access to the information on which the parole decision is based. Again both legislations make no such provision. This is not to say that an explanation is considered superfluous, but it is feared to cause considerable distress to certain prisoners, especially if the reasons which have led to a negative decision are beyond their control, e.g. their mental health or an unsatisfactory background.[13] We believe, however, that the detrimental effects of withholding an explanation will in the great majority of cases be worse than the distress caused by knowing the reasons. It seems incompatible with the principles of a democratic society that a decision to refuse parole should be made without giving the prisoner an explanation. Furthermore, decisions taken in private and according to no obvious principles, as is the case in England, can easily appear arbitrary. Surely it cannot be to the advantage of any parole system to heighten the ever-ready distrust of the prison population by a measure which, in this case, deviates unnecessarily from customary legal principles. The conflict, in our opinion, could easily be solved by giving full reasons to the majority of prisoners, and by making a more cautious statement to the few for whom the full reasons would be unbearable. It should be possible without insurmountable difficulties to find for these exceptional cases a formulation which is harmless in its generality. Of course, this would not be very meaningful for the minority in question, but it would at least allow justice to be done to the majority. Also, it would compel the deciding body to state the reasons for its decision more precisely.

(*c*) *The right to opt out* A third right of an eligible prisoner is worth mentioning: the right to refuse parole. Here again, the different correctional philosophies of the two pieces of legislation are revealed. The correctional ideals professed by the MPC obviously leave no room for any such right. When parole becomes a separate part of the sentence, the offender is left with no more choice of refusing than he has of refusing the prison term itself. Furthermore, there would be little point in opting out, for the only advantage the prisoner could gain would be a prolonged stay in prison without any corresponding benefit. The English prisoner is here, so to speak, in a better position. He is under no obligation to accept a measure which is still considered to be a privilege rather than a requirement. (LRC Rules 6[7].) Due to the different sentencing structure, the right to opt out may actually provide a realistic alternative, especially if the sentence is relatively short, as some prisoners prefer a discharge without supervisory restrictions, even if this implies a slightly longer period in prison.[14]

The parole period

1. Duration The conflicting approaches of the two systems in regard to the extent of legitimate correctional treatment becomes nowhere more evident than in the question of the duration of the parole period.

In England, as we have mentioned earlier, parole is not seen as a separate part of the sentence but as a modification in the execution of the prison term analogous to a transfer to an open prison or to a prison hostel. Consequently, the duration of parole may not exceed the total length of the sentence. For ordinary prisoners serving a limited term of imprisonment the parole period is even shorter, as the remission time for good conduct has to be deducted from the total sentence.

The English regulations as to the length of the parole period, impressive as they may appear at first glance because of their clarity and strict adherence to the length of the sentence, are not without weaknesses, the greatest of which, in our opinion, is their complete lack of flexibility. The parole licence has to remain in force either till the expected date of release or, in certain cases, till the end of the sentence. An earlier final discharge is not possible even if the parole period should extend over ten or more years. On the other hand, the statute allows for no extension of the parole period beyond the expected date of release for ordinary prisoners, not even if the parole term only amounts to a few weeks. The argument invoked in favour of these provisions is the rather weak one that a parolee, in respect of his final release, should not be in a worse position than a prisoner who has not been granted parole. The situation is aggravated by the statutory bar on release before one-third of the sentence (and not less than one year) has been completed. In the majority of cases, the actual periods of parole turn out to have been ill-suited to produce the intended correctional effects. They are either too short or too long. Experience has shown that the risk of reconviction is highest during the first two years after release with a steady decline after the first year.[15] Hence a term of approximately two years would constitute an adequate parole period. In the English system, this applies to very few offenders. In 1969, in fact, the average length of the licence period was about seven months, and of the offenders serving a sentence of over 4 years only 41.5% had periods of licence of one year or more.[16]

Parole should normally fulfil two important functions. First, to ease the transition from prison to normal life by providing practical help, e.g. finding accommodation, assisting with employment, etc.; secondly, to give the parolee continuous support and control over some period of time till he can manage on his own to lead a law-abiding life. With the present short licence periods parole is practically reduced to its first function. This may not matter too much for parolees with a good prognosis, but for others a period of supervision adequate to their needs may be a decisive factor in keeping them away from crime. In practice, the parole period usually proves to be too short, but it can occasionally turn out to be unreasonably long, especially in life sentence cases. England, as far as we can see, is the only European country to have an indeterminate parole period for indeterminate sentences. This may be very neat as a legal construction, but as a correctional device it seems out of proportion for the great majority of cases. One must remember that a life sentence in England does not really mean 'life' but is a misnomer for an indeterminate sentence, which can range from almost immediate release to life-long imprisonment for exceptionally dangerous offenders. The only rationale for an indefinite parole period we can find is to provide the Home Secretary with means of recalling at the slightest danger signal any person who has once committed a crime punishable with life imprisonment before he can commit another possibly serious offence. This is certainly legitimate, but it only makes sense for a small number of unpredictable or unscrupulous offenders. For the bulk of lifers, however, the risk of recidivism is not higher than for the population at large. For these cases, a fixed period of 5 years, for instance, would seem entirely sufficient and more appropriate than to expose them for a life-time to the strain of a potential recall of unlimited duration for any breach of parole. The same 5-year limit we would like to apply to excessively long determinate sentences of 15 years and over. As these sentences usually do not mirror the gravity of the offence but are given as a deterrent for others, it seems hardly justifiable to burden the prisoners in addition with an unnecessarily long parole term.

It is certainly not for its lack of flexibility that we can criticise the MPC's regulation of the parole period. If there is one main principle governing the determination of the time spent on parole it is the need of the offender. The mode of calculation has however given rise to some difficulties. Initially (Tentative Draft No. 5, s.6.09), the length was conceived as a function of the time actually spent in prison, the assumption being that the longer a prisoner had to be kept in prison the worse risk he was, and the greater his need for a long period on parole. By this means it was also hoped to create a double incentive for good behaviour in prison, as the prisoner's conduct could influence both his date of release and the time spent on parole.[17] The drawbacks to this proposal were considerable, the most important being the danger of lessening rather than increasing the prisoner's chance of going straight. In the case of a prisoner who had already served a prison sentence in excess of the usual quota for his crime, the addition of an equally long or even longer parole period could easily prove 'destructive'.[18] It was also feared that boards might purposely postpone release in order to lengthen the parole time. Fortunately this method has been abandoned in the Proposed Official Draft (s.6.10) in favour of an indeterminate parole period with a minimum of one and a maximum of 5 years in most cases.

The new solution – once one has agreed to abandon the English limits of proper correctional interference – seems almost perfect. It is flexible enough to give every prisoner a sufficient but never an excessive parole period, and it can be adjusted to individual needs irrespective of the length of time actually served in prison, since s.305.12 gives the Board power to 'dispense with or terminate . . . supervision.' An indeterminate parole term also has the advantage that it does not have to be fixed in advance but can be adapted to the parolee's needs as they appear during supervision. It is taken for granted that every prisoner should be discharged after the minimum if 'such discharge is not incompatible with the protection of the public' (s.305.12).

The American solution in its present form would hardly be acceptable for England since the 5-year maximum would in many cases exceed the length of the initial sentence. Yet, the principle of an indeterminate parole term could easily be adopted as soon as one would cease to consider the expected date of release as an absolute limit for correctional treatment. The minimum could then be fixed at the expected date of release or at 6 months, whichever expires later, and the maximum would be given by the end of the sentence, or 5 years, whichever is shorter.

2. *Conditions* (*a*) *Competency* The MPC does not raise the question of the competent authority to impose, vary or cancel conditions, since the power to deal with any aspect of parole is always vested in the board. Also in England (if our interpretation of the long-winded and not easily intelligible formulation of s.60 [5], CJA 1967, is correct) the determination of conditions of parole falls principally in the competence of the Board. However, the Board can delegate to the Home Secretary the power to impose certain conditions on any parolee or any conditions on certain categories of cases.

The conditions which the Home Secretary may include in any licence without previously consulting the Board are the standard conditions. These are automatically part of every licence, unless the Board explicitly changes or suppresses any of them. Four of the five standard conditions regulate the duties of the parolee towards his probation officer.[19] Number five is of a more moralistic nature and obliges the parolee to 'be of good behaviour and lead an industrious life'. No delegation has so far been made which would give the Home Secretary the exclusive responsibility to decide on conditions for special categories such as 'lifers'.

(*b*) *The condition imposed on parolees by the two legislations*

American parole boards have been criticised for establishing rules that are charged with moral and ethical overtones much more in keeping with the injunctions to a priestly acolyte or novitiate than the standards of reasonable behaviour for an actor in a complex modern social system. The authors of the MPC therefore thought it advisable to enumerate the permissible conditions as completely as possible in statutory form.

The limitations advocated by the MPC seem entirely sensible. They are outlined in Tentative Draft No. 5:

> The conditions of parole should be as few, reasonable and precise as possible. They should be of a nature clearly relevant to the parolee's conformity to the requirements of the criminal law. They should not intrude excessively or unnecessarily on the private life of the individual. They should be subject to clear and specific proof of violation (p. 104).

The way of drafting the conditions is also excellent. The central condition that the parolee refrain from engaging in criminal conduct has to be included in every parole agreement. In addition, s.305.13 enumerates a list of nine specific conditions plus a general clause entitling the board to impose 'any other conditions specially related to the cause of his offence and not unduly restrictive of his liberty or incompatible with his freedom of conscience.' S.305.14 authorises the use of residence facilities, such as hostels, hospitals, etc. In short, the conditions which can be imposed are clearly and carefully regulated.[20]

It is debatable, however, whether the individual conditions of s.305.13 always live up to the high standards set out in Tentative Draft No. 5. For instance, it is difficult to see how condition (a) of s.305.13, requiring a parolee to meet his specified family responsibilities, is normally 'of a nature clearly relevant to the parolee's conformity to the requirements of the criminal law'. We also consider well meant but rather naïve the condition to 'refrain from associating with persons known to him to be engaged in criminal activities or, without permission of his parole officer, with persons known to him to have been convicted of a crime'. This condition is not only difficult to enforce, but will inevitably be violated, especially by parolees who have always lived in an area with a high delinquency rate and associated with other criminals. But these failings seem of minor importance when compared to the advantages of an otherwise irreproachable list of conditions.

If we entertained some hope of finding similar statutory regulations in the English CJA 1967, we are soon disillusioned. Neither in the CJA 1967 itself, nor in a statutory instrument, has any attempt been made to spell out conditions. The subject was not even deemed worth a proper discussion during the parliamentary debate on parole. The only comment we can find is the incidental remark of the then Home Secretary, Mr Jenkins, who gave assurance that the conditions would be as clear and as precise as possible.[21]

We also look in vain for precise guidelines from the Home Office or the Board. The Notes for the Guidance of LRCs (part 1, p. 9) merely declare that 'conditions which would be difficult to enforce (e.g. refraining from drinking or gambling) should be avoided'. According to a Home Office view: 'The existing statutory powers to include conditions in licences place no restriction on the conditions which may be imposed . . . Any conditions imposed must, however, be reasonable. For example, the view has been taken that it would be an unreasonable use of power to require a licensee to leave the country and not return, and the policy has been to avoid attempting, through specific conditions, any meticulous regulation of the licensee's conduct.' The Parole Board, which is after all responsible for the formulation of conditions, is even less articulate than the Home Office. In its first report (1968), it deals with the problem in eight lines.[22]

In its second report (1969), the Board devotes some attention only to the special condition to reside as approved or as directed by the probation officer (p. 29). Again the principles guiding the Board are not discussed. Despite these theoretical shortcomings, the kinds of conditions actually imposed, with one exception, meet the standards set out in Tentative Draft No. 5. One could almost say that they meet them even better than the elaborate MPC legislation. The Board has so far considered that only five kinds of condition should be imposed. The parolee may be required:

(*a*) to place himself under the supervision of a probation officer (the special duties towards the probation officer are spelt out in the standard conditions);
(*b*) to be of good behaviour and lead an industrious life;
(*c*) to work and/or reside where approved;
(*d*) not to contact certain persons specified in the licence;
(*e*) to undergo medical treatment.

The only condition we consider unfortunate is the requirement to be of good behaviour and to lead an industrious life. The corresponding condition in the MPC simply asks the parolee to refrain from engaging in criminal conduct. Thus the code makes it clear that it cannot be the responsibility of parole to educate the parolee to a behaviour conforming to current moral standards. Its function is limited to prevent him from committing further offences. In our opinion, this attitude is the only defensible one, for there is no reason why society should be entitled to enforce higher moral standards in its parolees than in any other citizens. Society has every right to be protected from crime; it has, however, no claim to a moral behaviour beyond the minimum set by the criminal law. Bad conduct can be a danger-signal for possible further criminal activities. But the correlation is hardly strong enough to render the good-behaviour clause a condition 'of a nature clearly relevant to the parolee's conformity to the requirements of the criminal law.'[23] Furthermore, the term 'good behaviour' is so vague that it can be used as a convenient means to arbitrary revocation. It is surprising to find in a parole system as modern and generous as the English a relapse into the moralising tones of older legislation. More than twenty years ago, the old recognisance formula 'to keep the peace and be of good behaviour' in the corresponding section for probation (CJA 1948, s.3[3]) was already replaced by a version emphasising the crime preventing function of conditions.[24] Moreover, the courts in their decisions on revocation of probation, have tended to restrict the meaning of 'bad conduct' to actual criminal behaviour.[25]

The Home Office, as the orginal author of the standard conditions, has not only failed to follow suit, but for some obscure reason has considered it necessary to add to the good-behaviour clause the requirement to lead an industrious life.

The board although it has approved the condition, seems to interpret the term 'good behaviour' in the same restricted manner the courts do in the case of probation. The same can be said, as far as we can see, of the requirement to lead an industrious life. Sheer laziness is never made the basis for a revocation order unless it clearly leads the parolee to further criminal activity. It can be hoped, therefore, that in practice the condition will hardly have any undesirable effects.

The other four conditions are beyond reproach, and in some respects they are even superior to some of the requirements of the MPC. For instance, the condition not to contact certain persons specified in the licence has not, as the corresponding requirement in the MPC, the prime function of keeping the parolee away from undesirable company, but of protecting potential victims. An incestuous father, for instance, may be forbidden to see his children, or a violently jealous lover may be required not to contact the object of his former passion. In this form the condition remains easily enforceable and thus retains a real preventive effect.

Other conditions which we consider rather doubtful in the MPC, such as the condition to meet specified family responsibilities, have not been adopted by the English Board.

Evaluation

The strength of the MPC lies in its exemplary legislation and its impressive theoretical background. Even if we do not agree with all the conditions the American Law Institute has set up, we must recognise that the enumerative method used gives the parolee considerable protection against unpredictable fancies of the board. The English candidate does not enjoy this protection; he depends entirely on the Board's moderation and good sense. Should the Board decide to enlarge its present list of conditions in an unreasonable way, the prisoner has practically no alternative but to opt out. His chances of having the conditions altered by means of *certiorari* or by an action for a declaration[26] remain very small as long as the condition is not straightaway dishonest or utterly unreasonable. We do not wish to imply that it is necessary or even advisable that the CJA 1967 should contain a complete list of possible conditions. In view of the example of the good-behaviour clause we have some doubts whether conditions set up by the legislature really would be more sensible than the ones developed by the Board. The courts could already exert a reasonable control if the CJA contained only the few principles mentioned by the Home Office, e.g. that conditions have to be clear and precise, easy to enforce, etc. An amendment of the statute to this effect would leave the Parole Board free to impose any reasonable condition it deems appropriate, and yet it would effectively counteract any misuse of discretion.

Recall

1. *Competency*

All power to impose sanctions, as far as the MPC is concerned, rests with the parole board. Criminal courts have no recall power of their own even if the breach of parole consists of a new offence.

The CJA 1967, on the other hand, mirrors once more the English preference for splitting up the decision-making power among different agencies. These are the Home Secretary, the Parole Board, and, in addition, the higher criminal courts.

The division of power between the Home Secretary and the Board runs along lines similar to those already noted for the process of selection and creates no special problems. In ordinary cases, the Board makes the first decision. If it finds no sufficient reasons to justify a revocation order, its decision is final. If, however, it recommends recall, then the recommendation has to be confirmed by the Home Secretary (CJA 1967, s.62 [1]). In addition, the Home Secretary is granted an emergency power to recall a parolee without consulting the Board 'where it appears to him that it is expedient in the public interest to recall that person before such consultation is practicable' (s.62.2). Nevertheless the case must be referred as soon as possible to the Board, which decides in the last instance whether or not to uphold the revocation.

The relationship of the Board and the Home Secretary to the third recall body, the higher criminal courts, is less clear. If a parolee has been convicted of an offence punishable on indictment with imprisonment, the courts are granted the power to revoke a licence in lieu of or in addition to a fresh prison sentence. (s.62/6-8). Unfortunately, in giving the courts this power, Parliament was not aware that it implicitly granted the same power also to the Board and the Home Secretary. The grounds on which they can revoke the licence of a parolee have not been specified in the CJA 1967, but their general competency necessarily includes the power to recall a parolee for the most obvious breach of parole, the commission of an indictable offence. Since 37 of the 90 recalls made in 1969 were made for the commission of a further offence the question of who takes the decision is of considerable practical importance. Legally we have to distinguish two situations:

1. The alleged offence constitutes but one of several parole violations. For instance, the offender may have been also out of touch with his probation officer. In this case, a real clash of competency does not exist, as the Board always can recall the parolee on the other grounds.

2. The alleged offence is the only basis for a recall. Here, a conflict of competency becomes inevitable.

To avoid the issue of which body shall take action necessarily means solving it in favour of the Home Secretary and the Board, since only they can recall the parolee before sentence or even before conviction. Yet, we do think that such a result would be in accordance with the intentions of the legislators, nor do we consider it desirable.

The rationale of s.62(7) of the CJA 1967 was probably to give the judge the possibility of compensating lesser offences by revoking the licence for a fixed minimum period of time[27] instead of imposing a fresh prison sentence. This, obviously, can only be achieved if the Home Secretary and the Board do not make use of their power to revoke the licence before conviction or sentence. Another possible legislative consideration could have been to grant the recall power to that body which decides on the grounds for recall. In this case the courts should not only have a priority but the exclusive competence, as long as there is no other reason for recall.

On principle, as well as on practical grounds, we are much inclined to argue in favour of priority for a decision by the court. The disadvantages of a prior administrative revocation are numerous. They are especially evident in the case of a recall prior to conviction for the following reasons: first, when the Home Secretary and the Board revoke the licence before trial, especially if the parolee denies the offence, the recall is no longer based on a proof of guilt but merely on the surmise that the parolee is guilty. Secondly, the Home Secretary and the Board bar the parolee's right to bail. Thirdly, the time otherwise spent in custody is counted as recall time and therefore cannot be deducted from the new sentence (CJA 1967, s.67). Finally, the judge is deprived of the possibility of revoking the licence himself and may be forced to impose an additional prison term.

If the revocation order is made after conviction by a magistrate, but before sentence by quarter sessions, at least the recall is no longer based on mere surmise.

Early recall could only serve one positive purpose: to guarantee public protection in the rare case where bail is granted erroneously to a dangerous offender. There appears, however, little justification to argue for concurrent competency merely from such an exceptional case. All considered, we deem a solution of the conflict in favour of a court priority more appropriate.

The position that is actually taken by the Board and the Home Secretary is not quite clear. The latest recall statistics[28] seem rather to indicate that the court priority is not always respected. Only three of a total of 90 licences in 1969 have been revoked by courts, whereas the Board has recalled 34 parolees for the commission of a new offence. Presumably some of these parolees had violated their parole also in other respects. Unfortunately we have no information whether the offence was in all cases indictable, nor do we know how many cases have subsequently been brought to court. Even if we make due allowance for these possible exceptions, it seems likely that at least in a few cases the Board has made use of its recall power without waiting for the court's decision.

2. *The length of recommitment following recall*

Both legislations have shown an exemplary degree of moderation in determining the period of recommitment. The MPC has fixed the term in a clear and simple way in s.305.17: a parolee can be reparoled at any time; at the latest the board has to consider his case after the prisoner has served a period equal to one-third of the remainder of his maximum parole term, or after serving a period of six months, whichever is the longer; release becomes mandatory when the prisoner has served the remainder of his maximum parole term minus reductions for good behaviour.

Although the English legislation is not distinguished by a comparable degree of clarity,[29] in practice there has never been any uncertainty in determining the recall period. The maximum is given by the end of the sentence, or, for ordinary prisoners, by their expected date of release.[30] If the prisoner has served this period, he usually is released even if the maximum term imposed by s.62 (10) CJA 1967 has not expired.[31] There is no minimum period of recommitment other than for judicial recall. The prisoner can be released immediately. The rule, however, is that release is not normally considered till the prisoner's next ordinary review is due (after 10 to 14 months) or till his expected date of discharge.

3. *Reasons for recall*

If we need another example to demonstrate the different legislative concepts behind the two parole systems, there could be none more striking than the formulation of the reasons for which a licence can be revoked. The American Law Institute has considered it necessary to take every trouble to spell out precisely on which grounds a parolee can be recalled, leaving as little room for discretion as possible to the Board. The drafting of the recall section (s.305.15) has been particularly successful. The measure is limited to those offenders who cannot be dealt with by lesser sanctions, either owing to the gravity of the parole violation or because lesser sanctions would not prevent them from further violations: 'The Board may [only] order revocation of parole if it is satisfied, upon *substantial* evidence, that:

(*a*) the parolee has failed, without a *satisfactory excuse*, to comply with a substantial requirement imposed as a condition of his parole; and
(*b*) the violation of the condition involves:
 (i) the commission of another *crim*e (not just a misdemeanour); or
 (ii) conduct indicating a *substantial* risk that the parolee will commit another *crime*; or
 (iii) conduct indicating that the parolee is unwilling to comply with proper conditions of parole.' (s.305.15) [emphasis added]

English Parliament has shown considerably less preoccupation with the reasons for recall. The only reason explicitly given is the commission of an indictable offence punishable with imprisonment. We need not decide whether Parliament wanted to leave the regulation to the Board and the Home Secretary, or whether it considered the grounds for recall – the violation of a condition or the possibility of a further offence – sufficiently clear without statutory regulation. Whatever may have been the motive, its silence was certainly out of place. It means a blatant violation of the penal principle *nulla poena sine lege*, which says that the state has no legitimate authority to inflict punishment for misconduct that has not been previously and publicly declared punishable. This principle is no longer exclusive to countries with a civil-law background but has been increasingly accepted by the English common-law tradition.[32] It is equally valid for administrative sanctions of a clearly punitive nature, such as the revocation of a licence. The rationale is the same: to protect the citizens from unpredictable punishment. Under the present legislation, English parolees are denied such protection. Unless one is to assume that even the most marginal parole violation justifies a revocation order, they can have no certainty for which conduct they will be recalled.

Unfortunately, the comments of the Home Office and the Board do little to clarify the situation. The only statement the Home Office has produced is contained in a short paragraph in its memorandum *Life Sentence* (p. 7). It informs us that licences are usually revoked 'if some incident occurs which suggests that the offender cannot safely be left at liberty; and this may be either a further offence or some other disturbing course of conduct, such as threats of violence or failure to comply with a condition of supervision.' The brief comment of the Parole Board in its first report (1968, p. 11) is even less meaningful: 'The parole licence can be revoked and the offender recalled to prison if he fails to fulfil the conditions of his licence or commits a further offence while still on licence.' This is exactly the kind of vague definition against which the *nulla poena* doctrine was set up. It does not allow for any distinction between misconduct leading to recall and less grave parole violations. Moreover, it gives no warning that the licence can also be revoked if the parolee's conduct indicates the possibility of a further offence. Too many questions remain unanswered. We would, for instance, like to know whether the Board considers the dangerousness of a parolee in itself reason enough to justify a recall or whether he must in addition violate a condition of his licence other than to be of good behaviour. How likely must the commission of a further offence be? Will any threatening criminal behaviour justify a recall, e.g. also a minor theft? Only the last question is partly answered in the second report of the Parole Board (1969) in which it is stated that violations indicating only a temporary or minor lapse need not lead to a recall (p. 30). It can only be hoped that the next report of the Parole Board will at last specify the Board's recall policy.

4. *Sanctions short of revocation*

It fits well into the picture of general neglect with which the question of sanctions is treated in England to find that measures short of revocation have not even been considered by the legislator. Needless to say, in the MPC they have been extensively regulated (s.305.16). Basically, the code provides three such sanctions:

(*a*) a reprimand and warning;

(*b*) the imposition of new conditions or the more intensive use of existing ones[33];

(*c*) an extension of the parole period by forfeiting the reductions for good behaviour.

These are the typical sanctions short of recall provided by the parole legislation in most western countries. England, to our knowledge, is the only country in Europe which has not embodied them in statutory form. The Home Office and the Board have thus been forced to resort to measures which were laid already within their authority. Since the introduction of parole the Home Office has introduced warning letters, and the Board occasionally deals with troublesome parolees by making use of its power to impose further conditions (s.60[5]). Unfortunately, it is beyond the scope of either the Home Office or the Board to order an extension of the parole period, which, in our opinion is the most effective sanction short of recall. This could only be achieved by statutory regulation. Neither a warning letter nor the extension of conditions is ideally suited as a substitute for revocation in cases of minor violations. Warning letters have the disadvantage that they may not be taken seriously. Parolees who can be deterred by a simple warning are in general willing to comply with their parole conditions. The reprimand thus becomes a mere gesture to express the disapproval of the Home Office and the Board in cases where otherwise no action would have been taken at all. The extension of conditions, no doubt, will have more impact on a parolee. However, with the possible exception of an intensified supervision, the available conditions are so specific that they cannot be imposed at will on every parolee. They are therefore ill suited as a general sanction.

An extension of the parole period would be the only sanction short of revocation which is punitive as well as equally applicable to all parolees (except those serving a life sentence). There is, however, little hope that it will be introduced by Parliament as long as the current English views on the limits of correctional measures prevail.

The protections against unfair sanctions are unsatisfactory in both pieces of legislation. Neither of them provides for a judicial review, not even in the case of a revocation order. The Home

Secretary 'may revoke' (s.62[1]), and there is no remedy against it.

The MPC takes at least some precautions to avoid unfair sanctions by granting the parolee a hearing before the revocation order is made (s.305.15). Yet this right is granted with curious reservations. For instance, the parolee shall only have *reasonable* notice of the charges filed; or, the duty of the institutional parole staff is reduced to render the parolee not more than *reasonable* aid in preparation for the hearing. Still, he may advise with his legal counsel (if he has one), and he also may present proof, including affidavits and other evidence, in support of his contentions. In some American jurisdiction actual practice has gone beyond these provisions, judicial decisions having given parolees the right to counsel at revocation hearings.

Although, under the MPC, the position of an American parolee is not ideal, the situation of the English licensee is worse. He is not even granted the right of a hearing *before* the recall order is made. S.62 (3, 4) of the CJA 1967 only allows him to make written representations *after* his licence has been revoked, should he disagree with the decision. This legal construction of recall as a preliminary decision, becoming final if not successfully protested, may make sense in the rare emergency cases directly recalled by the Home Secretary. Over-riding security considerations can make it impossible to grant the parolee a prior hearing. But there is no sound reason why ordinary cases should be deprived of this essential procedural right. It would be wrong to assume that the denial of a hearing before recall can be repaired by the right to make subsequent written representations. It is well known that it is far easier to influence a decision before it is made than to change it afterwards. Furthermore, most prisoners are not experienced in formulating reasoned arguments and putting them on paper. And even if we suppose that a protest has been successful, and that parole has been restored, the damage which has been caused by an unjustified incarceration is not repaired.

The prisoner has to be given the reasons for his recall (CJA 1967, s.62[3]), but there is no obligation to give him notice of the actual information on which the recall decision has been based. He has no right to advise with his counsel, although the recall decision, as a judgement of guilt or innocence, would render legal assistance appropriate. In short, the statutory provisions are far from sufficient to protect the interests of a recalled parolee.

In practice, however, the position of the parolee is somewhat better than would appear from the statutory provisions. The LRCs, on their own initiative, have developed the practice of granting each recalled parolee an interview with one of the LRC members. A report of this interview is sent to the Home Office. Thus, the parolee gets at least some assistance in stating his arguments, and he can defend himself orally, although not before the body which decides on his case. It is unfortunate that the Parole Board itself has no power to arrange for an interview; this could only be granted by statute, as it has been done for the selection procedure. One may wonder why the CJA 1967 explicitly authorises the Board to interview parole candidates but makes no provision for revocation orders. Though there is little need for the first, the second would seem essential. The objection of administrative difficulties lacks cogency. The number of recalled prisoners is so small that they could easily be brought to London for a hearing before they are recalled to prison.

Conclusions

We hope to have shown the advantages and shortcomings of two parole systems based on widely different legislative concepts. A closer analysis has not made it easier, however, to decide which of the two is to be preferred. From a legislative standpoint, the parole section of the MPC is more adequate than its English counterpart. It is more comprehensive and it is formulated in clear and precise terms. Legal safeguards against unjustified decisions are guaranteed to a higher degree. More rights are granted to the prisoner, and the discretion of the board is more limited by statutory restrictions than in England. We do not know, however, whether the MPC would work out in practice more efficiently than the English parole scheme. The English system has two great advantages which could well compensate for legislative shortcomings. First, a board of experts which not unlike the Roman praetors, can correct and supplement the statute when necessary. Even if statutory guidelines are missing, it is likely that the Board with its high standards will reach decisions as appropriate as they would under the MPC. Secondly, compulsory correctional interference is limited by the extent of the sentence imposed by the judge, which is usually in a fair proportion to the offender's culpability. Thus, with the possible exception of offenders serving very long sentences, the negative effects of an unjustified refusal of parole or recall are never felt as strongly as under an indeterminate sentencing law.

Whether these two advantages of the English systems can make good for its statutory deficiencies remains doubtful. We shall know more if the parole sections of the MPC are enacted by American state legislatures, and when the English scheme has been established long enough to enable us to judge it by its fruits.

6 Some consequences of a parole system for prison management

KEITH HAWKINS

This chapter is based on research on the parole boards in four dissimilar American states carried out chiefly by means of interview and observation. American parole systems offer some striking contrasts with the English system, especially as regards the procedure by which decisions are made. Almost all jurisdictions, for example, allow eligible prisoners a hearing at their prison in the presence of some or all members of the state parole board, before a final decision as to the candidate's suitability is made. The provision for a hearing is probably the most noticeable difference between the English and American systems, and its existence has considerable importance for the way in which American systems are administered. But however parole systems are constituted, there are certain common features and common problems which are to be found in their day-to-day workings. The issues discussed here are by no means unfamiliar to prison staff and parole authorities in England.[1]

Parole is usually justified as one of the most important methods of implementing the correctional or rehabilitative ideal to which penal systems in England and North America are officially committed. According to the correctional approach, release on parole is considered to be 'largely dependent upon [a prisoner's] response to training and his likely behaviour on release',[2] while the supervision provided by an officer trained in casework skills in conjunction with the threat of revocation is alleged to contribute towards the further rehabilitation of the parolee. The parole board has a particularly important part to play in this view of the system, for it must decide which prisoners are suitable for release and also when parole should be granted. The correctional approach treats the latter question as one of great significance: 'the opportunity of supervised freedom at the right moment may be decisive in securing [the return of prisoners] to decent citizenship.'[3] In making either kind of decision, of course, a board has to come to some kind of estimate about the future behaviour of inmates if released. In this connection, the correctional approach suggests that board members should pay considerable attention to a man's general conduct and performance during imprisonment. Indeed, the White Paper *The Adult Offender* (in which the introduction of parole in England was proposed) went so far as to suggest, in a notably extravagant statement, that a 'considerable number of long-term prisoners reach a recognisable peak in their training at which they may respond to generous treatment, but after which, if kept in prison they may go downhill.'[4] The logical consequence of this optimistic kind of thinking is a very ambitious view of prison and parole as integral parts of what is sometimes referred to as a 'correctional continuum' in which an expert board makes 'diagnostic' decisions.

One implication of all of this is that what goes on in prison is officially seen as having a crucial impact on the workings of the parole system. At the same time, however, parole is almost always assessed in terms of the performance of individuals once released. Hardly ever is any consideration given to the consequences for the prison community of the presence of a system of discretionary early release by parole. In fact, with the occasional exception of the capacity of parole to reduce institutional overcrowding, official statements are reluctant to recognise that the system performs other functions in its inter-relationship with the prison or any other parts of the penal system. This essay considers some of these questions. To what extent, for example, are parole boards able to make decisions consistent with the rehabilitative approach? What kinds of clues do boards search for in the prison in making release decisions? Why use these particular clues? And what, in general terms, are some of the repercussions for a prison of the existence of parole?

The significance of control in prison

Whatever the precise penal policy adopted by or attributed to a prison system, the fundamental concerns of prison staff are to contain and control inmates. Custody is essential. There seems little doubt, as Sykes has said, that it 'looms largest in the eyes of [prison] officials'.[5] However, if this is the first objective, he concludes that internal order is a 'close second'.[6] Cloward holds a similar opinion; he refers to order and stability as 'the supreme custodial value'[7] [*sic*]. Only when inmates are contained and controlled can the business of rehabilitation begin.

If prison staff, then, are largely concerned with holding and controlling inmates, the chief task of members of parole boards is the release of prisoners. This is a substantial power and one, at the same time, ideally suited to the maintenance of control. There are two broad formal techniques of control in modern prisons: those which affect the quality of day-to-day life in prison (such as minor privileges and custody gradings), and those which alter the amount of time a prisoner must serve.[8] These techniques have generally supplanted cruder physical methods of control. One characteristic of this shift has been a greater emphasis upon the granting of rewards than upon the application of punishment. At the same time, adoption of inducements as a means of coercion to desirable behaviour has led prison staff to depend more and more upon the co-operation of their prisoners.

Remission and parole, both of which alter the extent to which an inmate is deprived of liberty, provide the two most important incentives to inmate co-operation. Both systems originated as means of assisting prison management, partly through aiding control, partly through their capacity to adjust numbers in custody.[9] The contribution of parole towards control in prison should not be underestimated. Prisoners, like the judges who sentence them, tend to measure the extent of their punishment in terms of how long they are deprived of liberty, and though the loss of liberty is only one of a number of deprivations they must endure, it is, as Sykes and Messinger have pointed out, fundamental to all the others.[10]

Remission is the more commonly used of these incentives, but its value would seem to be much more limited. It appears generally to have sunk to the level of complete routine in the United States (as in England), in which allowances are in effect given as a matter of standard practice and forfeitures made only when serious misconduct occurs. Parole, in contrast, affords more scope for offering incentives. In the first place, it cannot be taken for granted by prisoners in most states to anywhere near the same extent as remission. While it is true that some state boards release almost all their prisoners by parole,[11] a large number are still quite selective: on average about one third of those released from American state prisons are not paroled. Secondly, the legal structure of parole systems usually allows the possibility of much more substantial reductions to be made in the total sentence which any inmate may have to serve.

Though the first duty of parole board members is to make decisions about releasing people from prison, they must also have concern for the control of inmates in custody. While they may proclaim allegiance to the correctional ideal, they recognise that effective control and discipline are prerequisites to any rehabilitative efforts that may be made. Board members must also consider the reactions of news media, public opinion, and the consequent threat to their own futures[12] in the event of loss of control by custodial staff revealed in escapes, inmate violence or riots.

Parole policy vis-à-vis the prison community

The task of parole boards, then, is seen as one of making decisions consistent with the aims of the rehabilitative approach which will at the same time aid prison management. This leads board members to attempt to affect the behaviour of inmates in such a way as to satisfy both aims. Desirable modes of conduct are inculcated by the technique of reward and punishment expressed quite simply by granting parole to deserving inmates, judged by the standards of the prison, and denying it to others. The American parole boards can try to modify the behaviour of individual prisoners and at the same time use the decision as an example for the benefit of the prison community in general.

There are three ways in which boards can transmit their message to inmates. The first method, which can be used when boards interview prisoners, is to tell inmates directly why they have or (more likely) have not been granted parole. In the case of those who are not be released there is an implication that if they act in future in what the board considers to be a desirable fashion they will enhance their chances of being released. It is unusual, however, for inmates to be told with any precision either why they have not been granted a parole or what they must do to dispose the board to make a favourable decision in future. To do so may give inmates scope for protest, endanger staff-inmate relationships, and, perhaps of more concern to board members, embarrass a subsequent parole panel should an inmate who has modified his behaviour accordingly still be denied. The second method is to rely on institutional staff to provide their interpretations of the reasons for decisions. Finally, the board may leave it to an inmate to place whatever construction upon a decision he can, by using the knowledge generally available from other inmates and from institutional staff, and also by deducing from the matters discussed at the hearing and the apparent attitudes of the panel members what it is that concerns them. Inmates, however, do not like to have to put their own interpretations on decisions: it is too uncertain a method and makes them anxious and confused.

The parole decision is usually a problem of some complexity in which board members weigh up a variety of criteria. Sometimes they may base their decision chiefly on an estimate of a prisoner's risk to the community. In other cases they may wish to give overt expression to a value judgement as to whether or not parole is 'deserved', depending on the nature of an inmate's crime, his remorse, the length of time he has served in relation to his offence and criminal record, and so on. It is during this process of balancing conflicting criteria that parole boards also consider the implications of any decision for the intricate and delicately poised network of relationships they maintain with other agencies in the criminal justice system. This essay is concerned, however, with the effect of parole decisions on one segment of the penal system only, namely the prisons. The subject will be considered in three sections: the motivation of inmate behaviour, the maintenance of institutional morale, and maintenance of population equilibrium. All three are inter-related, and all three have a bearing upon the efficient management of correctional institutions.

1. *Motivation of inmate behaviour* Systems of discretionary release from imprisonment have long been administered with a view to control of conduct. Indeed, remission makes no pretence to being anything but a method of inducing good behaviour among prisoners (although historically its emergence and use has also been bound up with attempts to regulate numbers). Parole and indeterminate sentencing, however, have always been justified primarily as correctional measures, and the use of the parole power as a means of control has tended to be less conspicuous. The two aims have not been considered to be in conflict, for it seems clear that there used to be an assumption that good institutional conduct is itself a reliable indicator of reform. This assumption found expression in the composition of many early American paroling authorities, which were largely comprised of prison personnel. Even when these early boards began to be superseded by agencies independent of the prison, institutional conduct remained one of the focal concerns of board members. In more recent years, however, the correctional ideal has demanded a greater explicit stress to be placed upon criteria related to risk, while concern for control has become ostensibly less important. There are now varieties of treatment and training facilities available in present-day penal institutions and parole boards consider one of their chief tasks to be the application of treatment methods.

The importance of parole as a means of control is still evident, nevertheless, in both law and administrative practice. The formal shift in emphasis towards decision-making consistent with the correctional approach is nicely reflected in the present New York legislation which demands that

> discretionary release on parole shall not be granted merely as a reward for good conduct or efficient performance of duties assigned in prison, but only if the board of parole is of opinion that there is reasonable probability that, if such prisoner is released, he will live and remain at liberty without violating the law, and that his release is not incompatible with the welfare of society.[13]

Neither is the function of control abandoned by the Model Penal Code. One of the four conditions under which parole may be deferred is when '. . . release would have a substantially adverse effect on institutional discipline . . .'[14]. Another trace is to be found in jurisdictions which prohibit a prisoner who has had a disciplinary infraction recorded against him in the six months preceding his hearing from even appearing before the board. A rather similar practice obtains in the Federal jurisdiction where parole is not granted to those inmates who have forfeited their remission.[15] Two brief examples will be given to illustrate the importance given to control by administrative practice. In one state, the parole board receives a card which is kept independent of the parole files. This card lists any acts of misconduct by the prisoner who is appearing for his hearing; unlike the other information presented to the board, the card is kept absolutely up-to-date. In another state, disciplinary infractions are recorded in the case file on paper of a contrasting colour, to make them visible and easily accessible. Any brushes with authority are recorded, regardless of the fact that the prisoner may have later been acquitted or otherwise exonerated of the charges.

Parole boards are well placed to sanction institutional misconduct, since they are agencies of high status independent of the prisons. The remoteness lent by independence also means that board members can afford to be somewhat less worried about damage to staff-inmate relationships. But besides supporting custodial staff board members must also encourage inmates to devote themselves to their own self-improvement, as they must ostensibly make decisions consistent with the notion of correction. Thus as well as misconduct, parole boards penalise laziness or indifference among prisoners by denying parole, while giving the reward of release to those who have made conspicuous efforts in pursuing their own rehabilitation. On the other hand, they seem to expect good conduct as the norm. Thus those who have been particularly well-behaved can by no means expect to have this recognised by a favourable decision. In fact some especially compliant individuals may well invite a certain amount of suspicion if they give panel members the impression that they are adopting a tactic designed merely to impress the board. Equally, board members know that there are a number of prisoners who (either owing to personal inadequacy, or as a result of experience gained from previous bouts of imprisonment) are able to adjust very successfully to the demands and deprivations of imprisonment, but are less able to adjust to the demands of supervision and of life after release. But to grant parole to a perpetual troublemaker, or to a prisoner who has done little to change himself for the better, is seen by board and prison staff alike as a condonation of indiscipline or apathy. Inmates also resent the release of badly-behaved prisoners. Even though the board may consider them to be good risks release in such cases is seen by other inmates as an unjust conferment of a privilege.[16] In making exemplary decisions the board is of course trying to spread among prisoners and staff an expectation as to how it will act in the future. Its policy is framed around the general stipulation that prisoners offer more in support of their application for parole than mere adjustment to life in an institution.

Board members do not hesitate to spell out appeals to prisoners to cause no trouble. One case which was witnessed by the present writer involved a prisoner who had served a substantial part of his sentence for a crime of violence. He had plans for work and accommodation, if released, and the support of his family. He had a lengthy record of misconduct in prison, however, though there had been no reports of trouble since his last hearing. It was made clear to the inmate by the board that his misconduct was the only reason why he had not been released earlier. The chairman of the board congratulated the prisoner on his better conduct and on two separate occasions within the space of a few minutes told him that the board were quite willing to be 'conned' [deceived] so long as he avoided collecting disciplinary reports. This, the chairman explained to the prisoner, would give the parole board good reason to make a favourable decision. In the discussion following the departure of the prisoner, the chairman remarked that the inmate had 'kept his nose clean' for a year. 'He may be conning us about his good behaviour', said a colleague, 'But at least he's succeeding', was the reply. The board decided to grant parole. The chairman told the institutional parole staff that the prisoner should be informed that any subsequent misconduct would be treated very seriously indeed. Furthermore, a note should be sent to the inmate informing him that the board wanted 'exemplary conduct' from him for his remaining period of imprisonment.[17]

Most inmates, however, are relatively well-behaved. As a

result, parole boards are perhaps more interested in reflecting their commitment to the correctional approach by using their authority to ensure that inmates participate in programmes aimed at their rehabilitation – despite a lack of convincing empirical evidence to indicate the impact of these programmes on prisoners when released.

This is an important function of the parole power. Correctional theorists suggest that rehabilitative treatment and training is self-defeating if forced upon inmates; if rehabilitation is to be successful it must be undertaken voluntarily. The opportunity of early release by parole in fact provides a subtle compulsion which induces prisoners to engage in treatment, whether or not they personally feel it will be of assistance to them. Thus offenders, as Cressey has said, 'co-operate with correctional workers, not in order to facilitate their own reformation but in order to secure release from surveillance as quickly as possible and as unscathed as possible. Prisoners, for example, participate in group therapy, group counselling, and individual "intensive treatment" programs as much from a belief that doing so will impress the parole board as from a conviction that they, as individuals, need to change.'[18] In the same way, prisoners will act at their parole hearings in any manner which they feel will improve their chances:

> Johnson was nervous before the hearing. 'I'm wondering whether I'll say too much or not enough,' he had said, 'whether I'll put my foot in my mouth. If they ask me "Is this yellow wall blue?" I'll say, "Of course it's blue." I'll say anything I think they want me to say if they're getting ready to let me go.'[19]

The inmate who does not undertake treatment appropriate to what the parole board defines as his problem cannot expect a particularly sympathetic reception. A disinclination to undergo treatment may well be viewed as symptomatic of an underlying pathology, a reluctance to recognise shortcomings, hence a lack of 'insight'. The inmate who makes little or no attempt at treatment will probably find himself in a weaker position than one who has made mediocre efforts, or perhaps even one thought to have participated in treatment for the benefit of the board. Thus a prisoner known to be a heavy drinker was asked by the board how many times he had attended Alcoholics Anonymous while he had been imprisoned. The answer was twice. When asked why he had not made more of an effort, the prisoner replied, with a candour that in other circumstances might have impressed the board members as sincerity, that he did not believe the AA group was the answer to his problems. Parole was denied, the board members commenting that the man had shown little interest in treatment.

On the other hand, boards usually look more favourably on the prisoner who has spent his time in group counselling, in the workshop or in the classroom. So much the better if he has a variety of accomplishments to his credit. The importance of training is normally brought home clearly to inmates, for board members do not hesitate to draw attention to institutional performance in the course of questioning the prisoner at his parole hearing.

In attempting to motivate inmate behaviour by use of their paroling authority, however, board members face the difficult problem already referred to. How can they tell when an inmate has participated in treatment and training out of a genuine interest or concern? How can they see if an inmate has really subdued his troublemaking instincts and made a successful adjustment to prison discipline? It may well be that this distinction is irrelevant in relation to parole performance and behaviour on release, but the correctional approach and its emphasis on the notion of the importance of voluntary participation in treatment demands that it be given great weight. The only clues board members can use in answering these questions, apart from the assessments made by institutional staff which go into the parole dossiers, are those which they may pick up in their brief interview with the inmate. And because board members (and also the parole staff attached to the institution) usually give some indication to prisoners as to what kind of efforts are seen as virtually a prerequisite to release on parole, inmates are well equipped to deceive the board. Inmates know very well that boards are impressed with change and improvement; they are well aware that board members want to hear words like 'insight', 'maturity' and so on:

'Well, a young fella your age, it's a waste of time if you don't come up with some ideas about where all this is coming from and where you're going . . .'

Gardner answers slowly, the words measured: 'I know where it's coming from and I know where I'm going. I've done something to better myself in here. I've become an apprentice carpenter. And I've taken the time to think . . .'

Gardner is ringing bells with the board. He's done something to *better himself*. He may be *rehabilitated*. And maybe he is. He wasn't a carpenter when he came in. He was a thief, and not much of one. 'If they've got the tiniest bit of smarts they know what this board wants to hear,' an ex-inmate has told me. 'If you show some inclination to self-help, don't just do your time the old-con way. They want to see you run a little.'[20]

And inmates know that for change to be measurable by a board it must be explicit and visible. Ward has described one tactic adopted by inmates in the light of this. He reported that 'a number of inmates and officers have asserted, not altogether facetiously, that in order to show change you must "raise Hell" at first and then make a startling change and "go along with the program" . . . The inmate who is always a troublemaker or always a "model prisoner" cannot show anyone he has changed.'[21]

Yet prisoners who during the first part of their prison terms are badly behaved or indifferent towards rehabilitative programmes may later be regarded sceptically by the board, because they still run the risk that a subsequent change of heart may be interpreted by the board members as a mere device to impress them. Since the correctional view adopts the position that the genuineness of an inmate's efforts during imprisonment is related to his potential performance on parole, any conclusions drawn about an inmate's behaviour and sincerity assume considerable importance. A board has to make some kind of judgement of these during the brief parole hearing. This places it in an extremely difficult position. While board members insist on parole being earned, they know equally that 'inmates want out, and most of them will lie, smile or grovel to get out'.[22] This led one observer of parole hearings to conclude that 'as the hearing progresses, the suspicion grows that the entire process is an elaborate charade, a ritual dance honoring some dimly understood ideal of justice. Is it all a con?'[23]

2. *Maintenance of institutional morale* Board members must exercise a certain care in the extent to which they strike a balance between rewarding or sanctioning inmates. They are conscious of the fact that too great a readiness to defer or deny parole might largely remove the incentive for individuals to co-operate in prison treatment programmes. Perhaps even more important to a board, however, are the implications of too many adverse decisions for the morale of the prison population as a whole. Sentencing policy in many American states frequently results not only in high maximum terms being set, but also in lengthy periods between minimum and maximum terms, in which the parole board has sole authority to determine precisely how long any inmate should serve. As a result, board members are accustomed to thinking and dealing in years as often as in months. Deferrals for twelve months are common; periods in excess of a year not infrequent. Thus, while making exemplary decisions by means of their sanctioning power, board members must also try to avoid disillusionment, frustration and restlessness among those who remain in prison, and instead attempt to give encouragement and a sense of hope to the prison population.

This is no unimportant consideration. As a matter of efficient management, it is essential that prison staff enjoy the willing co-operation of their inmates. Those engaged in the work of rehabilitation also consider that the general morale in an institution is crucial in terms of shaping the attitudes of inmates to treatment and training and the enthusiasm with which they go about these programmes. In the words of a public relations document: 'A basic influence in the treatment program for the adult offender is the impact of the total institution upon the individual; that is, the institutional morale or rehabilitative atmosphere.'[24] Poor morale may also result in prisoners adopting attitudes particularly unfavourable to the parole board, institutional parole staff, and parole system in general. It is not inconceivable, though there seems to be no evidence one way or the other, that such men may be less co-operative with their supervisors if paroled.

Perhaps the most compelling reason why parole board members try to avoid lowering morale in the prison population is that control then becomes more difficult to achieve in an acceptable manner. Low morale raises tension in prison. Tension is a threat for it renders the community more vulnerable to friction which may in turn lead to escape attempts, violence or riots. In the compact, highly organised, frequently overcrowded setting of present-day prisons bad feeling is highly contagious. One prison warden interviewed said that it 'spreads like wildfire in the general population. It only takes few dissidents to have a general air of incipient rebellion within the institution . . .'[25] Any kind of disorder must be avoided at all costs: it represents a severe challenge to the established order which may take long to restore. It also usually provokes a great deal of adverse publicity which in turn raises public anxieties. This often brings the system into disrepute, and in those states where political appointments are made, trouble of this kind may threaten the jobs of senior staff.

Low morale in the prison population is easily provoked. Inevitably there will be some men who, for family or other reasons, desperately want to be released, however remote the possibility. Equally, there will be those prisoners who did possess some not unreasonable expectation of release, but whose hopes have been dashed by an unfavourable decision. But perhaps the more potent – though less obtrusive – cause of low morale in the general prison population is uncertainty. Uncertainty affects inmates both as regards the length of time they must spend in prison and also as regards the criteria which are likely to be considered relevant by the board in their cases.

The value of parole as a method of coercion to acceptable behaviour rests, however, upon uncertainty. The usual correctional view of parole as a system in which release is granted at a time most suitable for the furtherance of rehabilitation means that the power of choice is essential for a parole board. Such flexibility implies the threat of a relatively long term of imprisonment for inmates. As one parole administrator remarked: 'With this system, you don't fix the time. You keep [the prisoner] agitated. You keep him nervous. You keep him worried. You keep him wondering what's wrong with him. You keep working on this [for him] to get some insight. Then, when he comes up before the board . . . he's been working on his problems and he's better equipped to do something about them when he goes out.'[26] This rationale has long held great appeal for those who have advocated the correctional approach in general, and a system of indeterminate sentencing in particular. The logic which supports long maximum terms is here very persuasive. However, the longer terms become, the more vulnerable the prison population grows, and the greater the responsibility of the board in maintaining morale by giving as many inmates as possible the realistic hope that they will be released in the foreseeable future.

Some board members try to give inmates a sense of hope by direct encouragement at their hearings to persevere with their training, to behave impeccably, and so on. But the more important attempts to support good morale, however, are those in which board decision-making policy is diverted away from the ideal of flexibility towards greater predictability. Members of parole boards know that one way of preserving a sense of hope in the prison community is to keep a steady turnover of the population. Sometimes, for example, they may be more willing to release inmates held in institutions for the less promising to demonstrate that there is always hope of release. A change of board practice in the long term which results in fewer paroles being granted raises anxieties among the inmates. One board chairman said on this: '. . . I think every person in every institution in this state knows he's going to be paroled some time. He always has hope. And once you take away hope and you cut down on your paroles . . . this is when you have trouble.'[27] This pressure towards a certain predictability in decision-making also encourages the adoption by board members of a general principle that prisoners of similar records who have been committed for roughly the same kind of offence be treated in a similar manner. This principle is especially compelling if co-defendents are involved. Its application helps diminish a particularly potent source of inmate grievances, apart from satisfying the need to make the punishment fit the crime. Equality of treatment is a principle deeply ingrained into the fabric of institutional life; as McCleery, for example, discovered: '[i]nmates demanded, and officials asserted as a premise of prison life that all inmates must be treated equally.'[28]

Board members are themselves unlikely to be averse to making relatively predictable decisions though they may wish to preserve the illusion of a wide discretion. In addition to the fact that in doing so they create a certain tradition which serves as a useful precedent, some sort of standard response helps reduce their own anxieties in cases which are difficult to resolve: the observer of parole boards may well be offered words like 'tradition' and 'experience' in explanation of certain decisions. Besides, predictable decisions are not contentious decisions. Anything controversial tends to take time which most boards can ill afford. Thus decision-makers are not tempted to disagree with colleagues too often, lest their own decisions tend to invite argument, or even administrative review by the full parole board.

The second source of uncertainty which affects the morale of inmates is connected with the criteria upon which boards base their decisions. The correctional view of parole is premised on the notion that the attitudes and behaviour of prisoners may be changed during imprisonment. If parole is to be granted to those showing evidence of change, it is only reasonable to expect concern from inmates as to what kind of change is required and how it is to be manifested. While boards indicate in general terms what they are looking for, it is the absence of precise guidelines which worry and confuse prisoners. Board members do not usually make their criteria known to inmates, partly because decisions are often largely intuitive and also because some criteria are related to factors about which inmates can do nothing, such as gravity of crime. Board members also wish to avoid making any implicit contract with prisoners that if they alter their behaviour they will be rewarded with parole. Thus they prefer generalities: those prisoners who participate in their own improvement enhance their chances for parole. It is not usual, then, for boards to divulge precise details of what this means in a specific case, even if they were able to do so. But even generalities seem to inmates to carry an implicit bargain that if they do their training satisfactorily they will get out. Problems arise if these prisoners are subsequently refused parole. As one senior prison official indicated: '[The inmates] become all confused, and they say: "Well, I've brought the parole board every program. I've learnt a trade. I've got five years in group psychotherapy. The [psychiatric reports] say that I'm in good shape. Yet I'm still not going home. What is it they want out of me?" I think this leads to a lot of frustration.'[29]

Prison staff are not always able to advise inmates about the criteria which may be relevant in their cases, because they are often little better informed. They are sometimes reluctant to do so anyway in the event that they are proved wrong: 'When parole decisions are made which are obviously not in accord with what we tell inmates – what the staff tells inmates when they design a program – then the inmates are denied year after year, this gives the staff a feeling of frustration . . . It's difficult for the staff to explain to the inmate, because the staff may also have the feeling, along with the inmate, that the man has done everything he's been expected to do, and the time factors all seem to be satisfied.'[30]

But at least a system in which the paroling authority has direct contact with the inmate gives the board the opportunity to disclose criteria where it thinks this may be to an inmate's advantage. In the English system, in which the Board bases its decisions on written reports, inmates understandably feel the entire decision-making process to be remote and impersonal. The Parole Board has shown a certain amount of concern for the matter, and discussed it at some length in its *Report* for 1969: 'The Board wants to do all it can to explain its work to prisoners. Members have contributed articles to prison magazines, and during visits to prisons they have held discussions with groups and individuals about the aims of parole. It is not easy to dispel misunderstandings, for distrust of "them" is uppermost in the minds of many, and a few intelligent but embittered prisoners feed this distrust with misconstructions and discouraging comments. The Chairman of the Board answers many letters from anxious friends and relatives of prisoners and tries to clear up their doubts about the fate of their menfolk "inside" or the fairness of official decisions. Occasionally evidence reveals that these contacts have been helpful, even when parole has not been granted.

'Some prisoners may think of Board members as faceless or inhuman . . .'[31]

3. *Maintenance of population equilibrium* A somewhat different aspect of the prison in which parole boards are interested is the size of the inmate population. This consideration has a bearing on the maintenance of morale in an institution, for

manageable numbers ease the task of control. The capacity of discretionary release to reduce institutional overcrowding was a factor of great importance in shaping the antecedents of modern parole systems. Its capacity has also been explicitly recognised in England by the White Paper *The Adult Offender* which observed that parole 'would incidentally go some way to alleviate the existing overcrowding in the prisons.'[32] Since the beginnings of parole in England, however, the prisons have become even more overcrowded and it is not unreasonable to assume that this fact is largely responsible for more recent criticism that not enough prisoners are being released by the Parole Board.

Apart from the fact that keeping people in prison is costly, prison staff are inevitably concerned with institutional numbers because of the management problems posed. The notion that prison can be a place of rehabilitation is also endangered. Prisons do not have unlimited capacity to absorb inmates into their work, education or training programmes. The excess remain unassigned. Staff who would normally have been engaged in rehabilitative work may have to be transferred to surveillance. Moreover, as overcrowding increases, so does the likelihood of friction.

One obvious target for pressure to reduce inmate numbers is the court which sends them to prison in the first place. But even assuming that judges are by and large sympathetic to the problem – which is by no means always the case – sentencing policy and public opinion often demand institutional treatment for offenders. The laws in many American states also aggravate the difficulties by fixing the terms of imprisonment for given offences by statute, thus taking sentencing discretion wholly or partly out of the hands of the courts.

Because the parole board is close to the prison and not directly visible to the public it is suitably placed to effect some control over population levels. Board members, however, are understandably reluctant to acknowledge this. The warden of one large prison which held about twice the number of inmates for which it was originally intended recognised that it was 'not ideally the way to work' for parole boards to be more willing to grant release as a result of overcrowding. But, he added, 'The law of supply and demand certainly applies here. If we've got an overcrowded situation, the board looking at us would say,

"We've got to do everything possible to extend co-operation to alleviate the overcrowding situation." So I'm sure they will give the benefit of the doubt to people they might not ordinarily have paroled.'[33]

In considering the power of parole to regulate the inmate population, the question is usually treated as one of reducing numbers – the parole board is seen as a valve which opens to relieve pressure. There is some evidence to suggest, however, that boards may also keep prison populations up to a certain level in some institutions which have empty cells. Efficient management prefers the population of a correctional institution to rest in a state of equilibrium. Modern penal institutions depend heavily upon the labour and expertise of their inmates for their operation. As Paul Takagi has said: 'The inmates . . . represent the critical bodies needed for food processing, to fill classrooms, vocational shops, and the industries such as shoemaking, textiles, food preserving, dairying, road construction, and forest conservation. An implicit system requirement is to maintain population equilibrium.'[34] Cressey also hinted at this when he wrote: 'Guards and foremen who are to use work crews efficiently and to maintain peaceful routines, as well as treat inmates, cannot accept a system of discharges, job transfers, and other treatment activities that ignores the institutional necessities and operates solely on the basis of individual needs of inmates.'[35] In one state, for example, prisoners based in conservation camps carry out forestry work in conjunction with the state's Department of Natural Resources. The chairman of the state parole board has received communications from this Department indicating concern that some prisoners are paroled too soon – not that the men are considered unsuitable for release, but their departure reduces the labour pool and the Department feels that it does not derive sufficient benefit from its investment in the forestry training which it gives to inmates.

Conclusion

The prison is only one area in the criminal justice system with which parole boards have to support a reciprocal relationship. Decisions made elsewhere may affect the decisions they can make. The reverse is also true. Board members therefore also take an interest in sentencing policy, in the work of prosecutors, and in supervision and revocation practices, since their own selection policies may have an effect on the way these other decisions are made. The prison has been selected for discussion in this chapter since the immediacy and intimacy of its relationship with the board illustrate some of the latent functions of parole.

The fact of their interconnection, however, should not give the impression that relations between prison and parole authorities are necessarily always harmonious, or that board members are consistently sympathetic to problems of institutional management. The distinction between the basic roles – prison as a holding and controlling agency, parole board as a releasing body – should be borne in mind. Whether these contrasting roles give rise to strain and conflict depends on one hand on how committed a parole board is to the correctional approach and how willing it is to overlook institutional priorities, and, on the other hand, on the extent to which prison staff are determined to have parole decisions motivated by institutional considerations. Sometimes boards do not release men whom prison officials would like to see released, and sometimes do grant parole to prisoners whom the prison staff certainly would not wish to be paroled. The latter in particular tends to give rise to ill-feeling between the two bodies, since prison officials feel their authority in the prison is being undermined. In one state, for example, the Board had decided to grant a prisoner parole. Before his release, however, the man had been caught in an act of homosexuality. The Board nevertheless decided to go ahead and parole him. The warden was very disturbed at this decision, since he had recommended a further year's imprisonment, and he wrote to the Board chairman asking for the case to be reviewed. He complained that the additional month's sentence imposed by the board was insufficient for 'such a serious infraction' because 'it looks as if the administration and the Board are condoning active homosexual involvement in the institution'. The chairman, however, refused to be persuaded, considering that the punishment meted out by the institution for its own purposes was more than enough. Having emphasised that the parole board had the last word on the matter, he responded: 'the Board considered that the [inmate] had been punished by the previous institution action of being sentenced to twenty (20) days isolation, loss of custody from minimum custody to close custody, loss of his job, indefinite segregation, and further that he has a detainer [warrant] and will face prosecution in Federal court immediately upon his release.'[36]

Though parole boards possess the authority to override the advice or recommendations of prison staff, the latter are by no means powerless to influence decisions. The major part of the report available to the parole board, comprising evaluations and assessments of the individual's career in prison, is supplied by the staff of the institutions. The only contact board members have with inmates at the hearing may last no more than ten or fifteen minutes: otherwise they have to depend for their knowledge of the prisoner on what they are told by others. The role of the supplier of information in influencing decisions of this kind is an interesting topic for inquiry, but pending the results of research one can only speculate as to its importance.

The need to have regard to the requirements of prison management places a form of constraint on the free exercise of discretion by a parole board for correctional purposes. This typifies the relationship between parole and the penal system in general. Once a parole system has been introduced, it tends to show great durability – in fact the penal system soon comes to depend on the existence of discretionary release as a means of regulating the disposal and flow of offenders and also of preventing an uncontrolled escalation of costs. The value of parole in regulating the penal system is both more obvious and less open to dispute than its value as a means of rehabilitating offenders.

7 *Parole for the ex-prisoner: carrot, stick or illusion?*

J. IRVIN WALLER

Is parole effective?

Parole may be desirable to relieve overcrowding in prisons, or to mitigate severe sentences, but it is most often advocated as a means of protecting society by rehabilitating the offender. The annual reports of parole boards cite low 'failure rates' as if to suggest that these quasi-statistics represent a measure of the success, either of casework or of the deterrent effect of the threat of extra time to serve in the event of misconduct. In reality, the rehabilitative effectiveness of parole could be illusory. When other factors have been allowed for, it is difficult to find tangible evidence that either the 'carrot' of casework or the 'stick' of recall have much influence upon reconvictions, although they may well have an effect upon other aspects of an ex-prisoner's life. Casework is referred to here as a carrot (or reward) because it is meant to be helpful, although some offenders may look upon it as an imposition of unwanted medicine.

The results of research so far suggest that variations in penal treatments bear only a slight relation to outcome. For this reason, cost-benefit analyses have tended inevitably to favour the cheapest forms of treatment. Offenders themselves are also likely to prefer the cheapest treatments since these involve fewer restrictions. Probation or parole are cheaper than imprisonment, and absolute discharge is cheaper than probation. Fines and restitution are, in a sense, cheaper still, as they provide returns to the state or the victim.

Most systematic research done on the specific effects of parole has been carried out in California, and the task of evaluation of parole has proved to be very complex. The results are inconclusive, but they do show that parole supervision has much less effect upon criminal behaviour than many people would like to believe. Although vast sums of money have been spent on these investigations, a number of important areas of inquiry have not been adequately considered. For example, the fact that a parolee is an ex-prisoner has often been ignored. The parolee differs from the offender who has not been 'inside' in being the kind of person courts decide to send to prison. He must carry the after-effects of incarceration and of forced association with other criminals, and he must also cope with the difficulties of transition back to the free community. Examination of the supposed benefits of supervision has led to insufficient consideration of the deterrent effect of the threat of recall. Furthermore, criteria for recall have been very little studied, although use of the power to recall varies greatly between different parole supervisors and between different parole offices. Studies of parole from an economic standpoint have also been neglected, so that expensive forms of supervision which yield small returns are liable to be extended without regard to cost. In this chapter, while reviewing research into the effectiveness of parole, these neglected topics will come up again, for they are crucial to an understanding of the issues involved.

Although so much of the published details of experience and research come from California, and concern offenders on parole, the findings have been echoed in a wide range of studies of probation carried out in different countries. Practitioners in other places can no longer justifiably dismiss the conclusions of Californian research on the grounds that their parole systems have better methods of selection or differently trained supervisors, since these factors have been taken into account in some of the studies. Moreover, as will be shown later, the roots of the problem of parole effectiveness lie elsewhere.

There is one significant difference, however, between parole in California and in England which needs mention. California operates a system of indeterminate sentencing, so that the Adult Authority, which grants parole to prisoners, almost always decides when an offender should have parole rather than whether he should be paroled at all. Few prisoners in California with sentences over a year are released without some parole supervision. The parole board in California can delay the release in certain cases, but it has far less control over its failure rates than the parole board in England, which has the power to exclude altogether a large proportion of prisoners it considers unsuitable for parole. This is one important reason why simple revocation rates are not comparable between one jurisdiction and another. The English parole system can maintain a relatively small revocation rate by merely selecting out the poor risks, and leaving them to be released with supervision at the expiration of sentence. Indeed, the selection practice of parole boards has more effect on parole success than many of the other factors considered in this chapter.

The parolee is an ex-prisoner

The kind of person who may be released on parole is determined first and foremost by the kind of person the courts sentence to imprisonment. Prediction studies have shown that certain characteristics of prisoners are related to their post-release behaviour: age, current offence and previous conviction record are the most regularly cited of such factors. The more serious the offence, the older the prisoner and the fewer his previous convictions, the more likely he is to go straight after release. The predictive power of such factors is not very great, however, even when a much larger number are taken into account. While there is always great uncertainty about the outcome of any individual case, such factors may nevertheless be more important determinants of outcome than the presence or absence of parole supervision.

One would expect the offender's experiences during imprisonment to influence his behaviour after release. Early research studies did little more than obtain from parole officers information about reconvictions, or sometimes about the adjustment of ex-prisoners after release. More recently, particularly in California, parole administrators have interpreted their legal function to include the introduction of a 'treatment' element.[1] Accordingly, research has concentrated upon such factors as the use of group therapy, the size of the case-load,[2] or the use of the nalline test for drug abuse. But the impact of prison experience upon post-release behaviour has rarely been investigated.

This neglect contrasts with the fascination sociologists have shown, ever since the classic work of Clemmer,[3] with the study of inmate communities within closed institutions. Sykes, Morris and Morris, Mathieson and a number of others have studied maximum security institutions in North America, England and Scandinavia.[4] Polsky and Street *et al* have looked at some less strictly custodial and more treatment orientated institutions.[5] Students of sociology have been given a vivid picture of the clearly demarcated roles that are supposed to emerge in relationships between prisoners. The seemingly total power wielded by the 'wheel' or the 'tobacco baron', or the painful degradation of a 'fish' raped by a 'wolf',[6] or the simple but vicious process called prisonisation, are thought to have varying detrimental effects upon inmates.[7] But we do not know how these experiences may affect an inmate's behaviour on release.

Inmate role and post-release career

Some research has, however, focused upon the relationship between conduct after release and the role played while living in prison. But Glaser and Stratton have pointed out that difficulty arises because these inmate roles are not clearly defined. There is disagreement also as to the significance attaching to particular roles, and doubt about which role a given inmate played.[8]

Irwin and Cressey have suggested that the inmate culture is not caused by the institution *per se*, but is imported into the institution by the prisoners themselves.[9] On this view, the previous character of the prisoner determines both his role inside the institution and his behaviour after release. To investigate this empirically, Himelson and Takagi gave a number of attitude tests to California prisoners about to be released on parole.[10] They deduced the type of inmate role played by each prisoner from his expressed attitudes to staff and fellow prisoners. They found that inmate roles were related to whether a prisoner went on to complete his parole period successfully. However, since they also found that knowing the inmate role told them nothing more about the prisoner than they already knew from his history and characteristics on entry into the prison, knowledge of inmate roles did not increase the predictability of parole outcome.

It seems doubtful whether an inmate's relationships with others in prison are important to his life after release. The theory that inmate culture serves to develop close ties between prisoners was refuted by Daniel Glaser, who carried out an extensive series of studies of the US Federal Prison and Parole System.[11] He found that 58% of those co-operating in a follow-up study concerning experience after release had encountered other ex-prisoners during the first five months after release, but of these only 12% had deliberately planned to meet.[12] Glaser concluded that: 'Released prisoners apparently retain the cautious aloofness towards other prisoners, which we found they developed in prison.'[13]

One way in which the inmate culture might sometimes be important is in influencing an ex-prisoner to choose his friends outside from among other ex-prisoners. A 'choice' of this kind could presumably be largely determined by whether the offender has a wife and family to return to, whether he has accepting friends and relatives who are not themselves ex-prisoners, and whether he can obtain work in a place where he is not among others who have been in prison. These are all considerations unrelated to events within the prison. Indeed, the rift between prison life and normal society is so great that much of what happens inside can have no relevance to success in ordinary circumstances. In most prisons, for instance, work conditions are totally dissimilar from those outside. The inmate does not have to face the normal problems of obtaining a job, or coping with drink or drugs. If he has a family, his problems are not those of living with or supporting the family, but rather of trying to keep in touch with them.

A theory emphasising factors in the institution which may affect the prisoner's attitude to parole has been elaborated by Skolnick, who stresses the importance of appropriate attitudes and expectation towards release and the parole officer.[14] The theory may work for those who live planned and organised lives, but it seems unlikely to apply to the typical prisoner, who faces such an array of problems of survival on release that expectations about what is going to happen appear unimportant.[15]

Parole is a transitional status

Martinson, Kassebaum and Ward have commented on how little theory has been developed about the post-release behaviour of parolees.[16] One notable exception is the discussion by Studt on the successful re-entry of offenders into the community.[17] Studt classes parole as one of the many examples of changes in status that occur in peoples' lives. She points to the similarities between the changes involved in resettlement after discharge from prisoner-of-war camps or hospitals and the experience of parole. However, all the studies referred to by Studt imply that the individual is interested in achieving a new status and that, in the existential sense, he is free to choose alternative paths. In practice, a parolee may want to become a 'law abiding citizen', but he is not necessarily able to do this. He is likely to have to face a multiplicity of obstacles. His family may have become used to his absence and fail to give him emotional or practical support, or he may be at a loss to find accommodation or a job, especially if his previous work skills were limited and he now has to contend with the disadvantage of having a 'record'.

Garfinkel, Sarbin, Studt, and others, who have written about the relation between status and behaviour, have been especially interested in situations in which the individual finds himself ascribed a status that is negatively valued in society.[18] In California, as Studt points out, despite lip service to the notion of 'treatment', parole agencies see their essential function as one of control, and emphasise the need to be aware of the harm the parolee may do, particularly if he commits a sensational crime. The parole supervisor thus tends to class the parolee as a 'dangerous person' until it can be proved otherwise. He will require regular concrete proof that the parolee is employed, and living where he is supposed to live, but otherwise take little further interest in him. Further disadvantages of the parolee's degraded status may be that he must declare to prospective employers that he is on parole, or he may be unable to obtain a driving licence without special permission. The parolee may also suffer in less overt ways such as when the supervisor defines parolees as persons unable to take decisions. These disadvantages of the low status ascribed to parolees can seriously impede their adjustment to normal society.

Parolee and parole supervisor

Research on the correctional effectiveness of parole has begun to change, moving from its original concentration on prediction of reconviction, to include more descriptive and experimental studies, taking account of variations in organisation of case-loads, and noting their apparent influence upon violation rates. One needs to look at the findings rather critically. After all, parole is a form of compulsory casework, and the results of research elsewhere suggest that such casework is not an effective method of reducing recidivism.

The classic random allocation experiment is supposed to be the soundest test of the effectiveness of parole supervision. In such an experiment, two or more types of supervision or treatment are provided, and an unselected series of parolees are allocated at random to one or another of the treatments. This procedure avoids the bias that could occur with a human decision-maker who might unknowingly select the more promising men for a particular treatment. Experiments of this kind have been carried out in California for nearly twenty years. The clear conclusion to be drawn from them is that more intensive parole supervision does not produce major reductions in reconviction rates. In one piece of research (Phase III of the Special Intensive Parole Unit project)[19] some differences were observed suggesting that smaller case-loads were more effective, especially in the case of the parolee who was neither a very good nor a particularly bad reconviction risk. Unfortunately further work (S.I.P.U., Phase IV)[20] failed to confirm the result. In any event it is difficult to see any logical reason why 'average' types should be especially amenable to individual casework. One might logically expect the high risk group to be more responsive to increased attention, especially if it involved intensive 'police' type supervision likely to deter them from further crime.[21]

Differential treatment

Ever since 1959, when Grant and Grant published their observations on the treatment of US naval delinquents,[22] the apparent ineffectiveness of penal treatments has been explained by the theory that any particular method is liable to make some people better and others worse. Researchers have tried to classify both treatments and offenders in order to identify the different regimes best suited to different cases. A classic example of research designed to match different kinds of offenders with different types of treatment approach is the California Community Treatment Project of the California Youth Authority. Some of the results of the Project do suggest positive effects due to treatment, but in general the conclusions are still uncertain. The investigators have relied upon technical violation rates as a measure of success, but these are unsatisfactory.[23] Comparisons using more objective criteria, such as convictions for felony, have so far given less encouraging results.[24] One finding of the Community Treatment Project, although it has nothing to do with the effectiveness of supervision, has a bearing upon the value of parole; it was demonstrated that early release did not result in increases in major arrests.

The Community Treatment Project also tried to measure other effects of treatment than reduction in convictions, notably family adjustment and school performance. No analysis of the results of these comparisons have yet appeared, although it is obvious changes in these other aspects of behaviour could well reveal important effects of treatment, and so remove some of the uncertainties in the conclusion on the effectiveness of the project.

Hood and Sparks have reviewed critically a number of other studies purporting to show the differential effect of types of treatment upon different types of offender.[25] Several of the studies failed to demonstrate any significant differential effects, but the California Pilot Intensive Counselling Project did find consistently better results when treatment was given to a particular amenable group.[26] A study by Hall and others, which claimed to have found differential treatment effects with adult prisoners, furnishes typical example of the problems encountered in this kind of research.[27] The statistical evaluation that was used (a base expectancy method derived from configuration tables),[28] is one that 'capitalises on chance'. Without repeating the observations and obtaining similar results one cannot be sure the findings were not spurious. Even though the research workers themselves pointed out the need for replication, they still suggested that the differences they found were probably due to the treatment programme.

In attempts to advance from the slight and tenuous nature of the findings so far reported, both for institution and community treatments, the search for differential treatment effects continues, and indeed has become the mode for both research and administrative programmes, especially in California. Despite many methodological difficulties, these researches may yet bear fruit.

Meantime, the main programmes of treatment introduced in recent years, such as the Special Intensive Parole Unit, and the California Work Unit, make use of different regimes for different offenders. But instead of classifying offenders by treatment needs, they allocate on the basis of risk or reconviction.[29] Even in the Community Treatment Project, where the classification of offenders was supposed to be based on treatment considerations, highly intensive supervision may be seen to be allocated primarily on the basis of risk of reconviction; it appears that those high risk offenders who would normally have to be sent to institutions must be supported in very small case-loads in order for the community to tolerate innovation. In the case of adult prisoners one wonders why such programmes still have to be justified by pretending that differential rehabilitative treatment is being applied. It would be simpler to admit that people like to keep closer tabs on offenders who are greater reconviction risks. It may be that the public has been led to believe that prison 'protects' them for so long, that now we cannot turn round and let criminals 'free' without intensive supervision for the sake of the illusion of protection which this provides.

Numbers and 'significance'

The likelihood of being able to demonstrate statistical significance in an experiment depends upon the size of the sample. If the effect of a treatment is small, a large sample will be required in order to show statistical significance. Conversely, if the sample is very small, only very large effects will produce significance. It is often overlooked that a positive but statistically insignificant effect in a small sample may be of greater economic importance than a statistically significant result from a very large sample.[30] In the report of Phase III of the Special Intensive Parole Unit there were 911 parolees supervised intensively in small case-loads compared with 2,806 supervised in regular case-loads. The difference, in terms of percentage arrested, is shown in Table 7.1.

Table 7.1

Percentage of small case-load and regular case-load parolees arrested in a 12 month follow up

Parole outcome:–	No Arrest	Minor Arrest	Major Arrest	Return to Prison	Total
Small Case load	42.0	20.6	13.0	24.4	100%
Regular Case load	37.2	22.5	12.0	28.3	100%

This difference in distribution of parolees among the four outcome categories is statistically significant,[31] but the size of the effect is too small to be economically useful. The small case-loads were 35 per officer, approximately half the regular case-loads, and the number of persons arrested was 5% less for small case-loads than for large case-loads. With a total of 3,717 parolees, to achieve a 5% decrease in arrests, about 50 additional parole officers would be needed. In terms of cost-benefit, the cost of the additional officers might exceed the cost of the (185) arrests prevented. This schematic analysis is meant merely to illustrate the point that a statistically significant effect may or may not be important according to the values and costs involved. Using a much more sophisticated analysis, employing a system model of criminal justice administration, the repercussions on other aspects of the system of halving the parolee case-load could be seen more clearly, and rational changes could be made more easily.[32]

The important point is that a small but significant treatment effect in an experimental study is only likely to appear if large numbers of individuals are involved. In the San Francisco project, where there was only a small total of 307 parolees involved, who were distributed between minimum (118 cases), ideal (119 cases) and intensive treatment (70), it is hardly surprising that the researchers were unable to find differences in outcome of statistical significance.

Table 7.2 displaying the San Francisco findings, provides evidence that the number of technical violations are greatly affected by type of supervision, but shows little else. Unless controls are applied to check upon the discretion of the parole supervisor in deciding what behaviour constitutes a violation, and unless the period at risk – the time from release during which an arrest could occur – for different parolees is equated, no firm conclusions can be drawn. The statistics may indicate more about the administrative decisions of the parole agents than about the behaviour of the parolees.[33]

Table 7.2

Violation Rates: San Francisco Project Case-loads[34]
Northern District of California

	TYPE OF CASE-LOAD		
	Minimum: Sept. 1964- Aug. 1966	Ideal: Sept. 1964- Sept. 1966	Intensive: Sept. 1964- Nov. 1966
Number of cases under Supervision:	118	119	70
Number of Terminations:	18	37	32
Number of Successful Terminations:	14	28	20
Number of Warrants:			
Total:	4	9	12
Based on new offence:	4	8	5
Based on technical violations:	0	1	7
Violation Rates:			
Total:	22.2	24.3	37.5
New Offence:	22.2	21.6	15.6
Technical Violations:	0.0	2.7	21.9
Excluding technical violations from compstations:	22.2	22.2	20.0

Empirical studies on the decision to revoke parole

Takagi and Robison have demonstrated wide variations, both between individual parole *officers*, and between different parole *offices*, in regard to their decisions to revoke.[35] By presenting for judgement ten actual case histories taken from parole files,

Takagi was able to show that recommendations for return to prison varied significantly not only between individual parole officers, but between officers of different status, and between different types of parole office. Perhaps this is not surprising. Even in the courts, where procedures are designed to protect the rights of the accused, and even where appeals against sentence are possible, enormous disparities in sentencing have been shown to occur between different magistrates.[36] Some of this variation depends upon whether the magistrate comes from a rural or urban community, and upon his socio-economic background, and even upon which court of the same court house he works in. In spite of the long periods of custody that may be involved, in the case of parole revocation decisions the prisoner's rights are unprotected and erratic variations are not so unexpected.

Takagi was able to show that some of the variation in recommendations for revocation of parole was because case needs received most emphasis in one parole unit, whereas another laid more stress on maintaining standards.[37] The significance of his results from a rather small sample indicate the importance of the considerable variations that can occur. Takagi's findings cast further doubt upon the conclusions from the large-scale case-load research of the Special Intensive Parole Unit which was mentioned earlier. In that project their results were significant only with large numbers of parolees, and no checks were made on the nature of the decisions by the parole agents involved. Since Takagi has shown that agents can vary enormously in this respect, such variation might account for the slight differences of outcome observed between the smaller and larger case-load groups.

Technical violations can be affected by administrative fiat.[38] Takagi set out the history of one agency to which money was allocated by a state legislature to enable supervisors' case-loads to be reduced from 70 to 35. Early evaluation failed to show the expected reduction in violation rates, but the agency felt that they needed to justify the enormous amount of funds they had been allocated. The chief administrator therefore called a meeting of his colleagues, and deliberately set about achieving lower violation rates. The supervisors involved in small case-loads were required to hold a conference with their superiors to see what could be done to avoid returning parolees to prison. Each supervising unit was to compete against the others to see which could produce the lowest technical violation rates. Future promotions of senior personnel could be considered in terms of how well they had provided leadership in reducing the technical violation rates.[39] A year later, the resulting research report was able to show reductions in recommitment to prison among the parolees supervised in small case-loads. However, the numbers of parolees supervised in conventional size case-loads who were recommitted to prison were also reduced.

When the supervising parole officer is made aware of a violation, his recommendation initiates official parole agency reaction and thus appears to be an important determinant of the ultimate revocation decision. It seems to be rare for a parole board not to accept a recommendation to revoke parole, and Takagi has shown that, in one state at least, such recommendations are largely those made by the parole agent. In an examination of 1,700 emergency cases reported by the parole agents in a single region in 1963, Takagi found only thirteen cases in which the parole agents' superiors disagreed with the original recommendation.[40] Similar findings are reported by Robison concerning decision to discharge offenders from parole.[41] However, it is important to note that parole agents' recommendations may themselves be heavily influenced by the views of their administrative superior.[42]

As Ward has pointed out, negative findings in evaluative research may have long-term repercussions.[43] For example, the publication during the third phase of the Special Intensive Treatment Unit project of the negative findings of the first two phases might have affected the study situation. It could have encouraged parole agents to better and more effective work, or it could have led to a policy of leniency in marginal cases of violation.[44] It is impossible to tell whether these hypotheses apply to Phase III, but both are consistent with the findings. In Phase IV some validation of the earlier work was possible. In an analysis of the results of Phase IV, taken together with the earlier findings, Havel came at first to the same conclusion that smaller case-loads do have some real effects upon the behaviour of parolees, but whether small case-loads give better results depends on the criteria of 'success'. Apparently small case-loads help to keep men free of arrest but do not prevent return to prison. However, even Havel's modest conclusions about differential effectiveness disappear when comparisons are made after grouping the parolees into risk categories on base expectancy scores.[45]

Tentative conclusions about the effectiveness of correctional treatments

Having described some examples from the growing literature of research on the effectiveness of parole it is possible to form some impression of the trend of the findings. Adams, and Hood and Sparks have reviewed some general conclusions.[46] One of the most important omissions in most research so far has been the failure to consider any criteria of effectiveness other than those relating to re-arrest. Parole supervisors interested in helping 'clients' are quick to point out the extraneous factors that effect arrest histories, and to suggest that arrest does not really measure the success of rehabilitative work. Apart from the shortcomings of re-arrest as a measure of behaviour, it is probable that the true effectiveness of a treatment programme can only be understood by considering other kinds of outcome.

So far as they go, the findings of research point to two alternative hypotheses. Compulsory parole supervision in the community has no effect on an offender's chances of reconviction, or, alternatively, it has too small an effect to be of economic importance. If, in addition, one takes note of the work on variation in revocation decisions, the likelihood that existing treatment programmes have any substantial effect in reducing crime seems even less. Finally, if cost to society is considered, it appears that the extra money invested in these schemes yields an insignificant return.

Influence of revocation and rule enforcement

Another interesting omission in contempory research is the lack of comparisons between new treatments and no treatment at all. For instance, in the research on case-load variations, few studies compare men released under varying degrees of parole supervision with those released without parole.[47] Likewise, few studies compare offenders on probation with offenders conditionally discharged without supervision. Even in the San Francisco project, which purported to show that minimal supervision was as effective as more intensive supervision, the minimum supervision group was still subject to the rules and regulations of probation and parole, and therefore liable to revocation. We really know very little about the influence of living under threat of recall to prison as opposed to release without parole.

An important aspect of parole is that if the parolee is caught and convicted for another offence, or if he is recalled for a technical violation, he is liable to serve some sizeable proportion of the remainder of his prison sentence. The potential severity of this penalty, and the way it is calculated, vary greatly between jurisdictions. Such variations are important, since this is a threat that seems likely to have some influence upon many areas of a parolee's life. For instance, a parolee may make more effort to obtain and keep a job because he sees this as a way of maintaining his freedom. Similarly, it would be foolish to imagine that a parolee reports regularly to his supervisor solely because he feels he benefits by the experience. Nevertheless, in both instances the parolee is conforming to the rules.

An alternative *modus vivendi* for the parolee is to pretend to conform by seeing to it that the parole supervisor and the police receive only 'appropriate' information. The parolee may tell the supervisor about problems that he knows the supervisor would like to hear, while avoiding topics that might lead the supervisor to become suspicious. Most contacts with the supervisor probably take place in his office, and in this setting it is easy to paint a picture different from the truth. Moreover, even in supposedly intensive supervision in small case-loads, the supervisor rarely spends more than an hour a month in face to face contact with the parolee. Even where regulations (such as those of the Work Unit in California) require the supervisor to make some contacts outside the office, it is still relatively easy for the parolee to disguise what he is doing.

Some studies have been carried out to see how parole supervisors spend their time, and how they redistribute their activities when case-loads are reduced.[48] The findings of all these studies point to the same general conclusion. Reduction in case-load by as much as half, for instance from 70 to 35 parolees per supervisor, does not bring about any great change in the way supervisors distribute their time between different activities. In particular, the proportion of their time spent in face-to-face contact remains the same. The explanation for this seems to lie in the carry over of work habits geared to larger case-loads. The result is that surveillance remains fairly minimal. As Robison has pointed out,[49] a supervisor with a 40 man case-load, who spends 25% of his working time in face-to-face contact with parolees, would still average only one hour per month with each client, and from the studies cited above even that could be an overestimate. Moreover, the schism between the hundreds of hours of day to day living, when the parolee is not under surveillance, and the one hour of direct contact, is much more than a matter of length of time. In a participant observation study of a sophisticated residential training school for delinquent boys, where treatment by individual interviews was in operation, Polsky has noted: 'In a short walk from the clinic to the cottage the boy passes from one society to another.'[50] This observation [pointing to the gulf between living circumstances and the potential for either treatment or surveillance of the office interview] is even more pertinent to offenders on parole.

Parole licences in the North American systems are permeated by a large number of specific prohibitions, such as total abstention from intoxicating liquor, from associating with undesirables, from use of narcotics, from gambling, from possessing a gun, from incurring debts and so on. These onerous requirements discourage parolees from being frank with supervisors. So-called intensive supervision is supposed to prevent deceptions, but it is open to question to what extent it really succeeds in altering the offenders' life styles, or merely results in more sophisticated game playing. Some of the rules are based on criminological ideas of what keeps men from crime. Studies have shown that men who are employed are less likely to be involved in crime, but it is not clear whether it is the characteristics of the men who become unemployed that leads them to crime, or whether it is the actual state of unemployment that provokes them to crime. The requirement to work or to 'lead an industrious life' may press gang parolees into taking up jobs, but the effect of this on their propensity to criminal behaviour remains uncertain.

There are considerable differences in the extent to which parole conditions are enforced by supervising officers, which must lead to varying ideas among parolees as to which rules are important. This in turn must lead to an unstable balance between game-playing and genuine changes in habits. The English parole licence, with its general requirement of good behaviour, but absence of specific rules, has been praised in North America.[51] However, under any system, the actual standards enforced are what parole officers decide, subject only to the general boundaries drawn by parole boards when they make recall decisions. In practice, limits are negotiated between parolee and supervisor. A number of American studies have shown that few of the technical violations that come to the notice of supervisors actually result in recall.[52] The interaction between parolee and supervisor is important to an understanding of the potential influence on the parolee's life style, although the influence may be more through threat than casework, brought about more by the 'stick' than the 'carrot'.

Over-concentration of research upon the casework relationship has led to neglect of other influences on success rates. One of the most important findings to come out of the San Francisco project was in a non-experimental section in which offenders who completed their probation or parole successfully were asked their views as to the contribution of supervision to their success. In general, it appeared that the part played by family and associates was more important than the activity of the supervisor. This seems obvious, and yet research has tended to concentrate on the effects of changes in intensity and methods of supervision to the neglect of other aspects of the parolee's environment, such as parole restrictions or coercion to take a job.

One of the few researches upon the effects of coercive casework was concerned with 'Enforced Clinic Treatment of Paroled Criminal Alcoholics'.[53] Since earlier work had shown the importance of alcoholism among offenders released from state penitentiaries, and since alcoholism is believed to be a factor in crime, the need for such an experiment is obvious.[54] The size of the sample was small (only 19 male alcoholics paroled) but statistically significant results emerged in relation to recidivism and other criteria. This suggests that an important method of treatment has been discovered which warrants fuller investigation with larger samples. This result suggests further that, if reduced case-load size is to have an effect in reducing recidivism, it must be accompanied by some effort to identify and deal with each parolee's specific problems.

In this discussion of the effects of the coercive element in parole many questions remain unanswered because the necessary empirical research has not been done. It is, however, an important area, in which the formulation and testing of hypotheses is badly needed.

Conclusion

If we think of the assistance provided by the parole supervisor as the 'carrot', the evidence so far suggests that this is of minor importance in affecting the criminal behaviour of parolees. The question still remains, however, as to what extent the supervisor may help the parolee in other respects, for instance in finding and keeping a job, in resolving marital disputes, in lending money, in finding accommodation, or in providing the friendly 'listening ear'. As regards the threat of revocation, and the effect of deterrence generally, that is the element of the 'stick', too many questions remain unanswered. The parolee may be coerced into a greater effort to fulfil social requirements, or he may be stimulated to fool his supervisor.

But despite all the repetitive discussion about measures of success, reconviction must remain an important criterion in assessing the effectiveness of sentences and penal treatments. In understanding the outcome of releases on parole, the most important elements appear to be the selection policy of the parole boards, the offender's previous history, the offender's behaviour after release, and the reaction to it by parole supervisor, police and public. Finally, and possibly more important than the rest, this outcome is subject to a whole range of chance events and decisions that defy deterministic analysis.

This chapter has attempted to introduce a note of realism in regard to the effect of parole in changing behaviour. This is not necessarily to challenge its *raison d'être*, but it has been beyond the scope of this chapter to discuss other positive reasons why parole should exist. Such reasons are the concern of those who must deal with such problems as the cost of new prisons, the relief of overcrowding, and the need to placate public opinion with the claim that justice is being done and protection being given, even though criminals are being set free.

These sceptical conclusions may leave the parole officer feeling that he is being used by the system without being able to accomplish anything constructive. He may challenge the conclusions because he can recall some cases in which he felt that he was instrumental in successful rehabilitation. It is not denied that a supervisor may play an important role in the lives of some parolees, although examples are rarer than the casework literature would lead one to believe; but if the supervisor had not played the role in question someone else might have done so. Supervisors may make life more comfortable for the parolee, and may help him with his personal troubles, but this does not seem to have much bearing upon recidivism, except, perhaps, where the parolee's problem (e.g. alcoholism) is one that leads to recidivism unless it is resolved. Until descriptive work has identified specific problems in the parolee's situation, independently and importantly related to outcome, such as drink, unemployment, associates, or family relationships, vast experimental projects will be unlikely to yield much result. When these more specific topics have been studied, it may be possible to find a positive role for the supervisor to play, and to suggest how supervision might be redirected to combat these particular problems.

Instead of concentrating upon casework, it could be that effort would be better directed towards the provision of sheltered workshops, or compensation to employers willing to take an ex-prisoner, or simply the promotion of more community tolerance. Alternatively, it may be, as Robison has suggested, that money is being squandered on 'corrections' when it could be used more effectively in 'prevention'. Belief in the panacea of the probation or parole 'relationship' has swept England and California, and may sweep through Europe and other parts of North America. Now it is time to stop trying to prove that this easy 'cure all' will work. Parole was not a rationally thought out solution, and the measures advocated are expensive in dollars and lives. The time has come to stop and think and try to understand.

This chapter has dealt with the effects of parole, but parole is only an adjunct to imprisonment. If parole is just a cheap, humanitarian stick, and its effects possibly illusory, what then is prison?

8 *The assessment of risk in parole decision making*

VINCENT O'LEARY and
DANIEL GLASER

When a parole board member decides whether to parole an inmate, his decision usually involves a balance among a variety of considerations. Almost always he reaches some judgement as to what the prisoner's behaviour will be on parole. He may also consider what the public's reaction is likely to be as well as the possible reactions of institution staff and inmates to a given parole action. The attitude of the courts and police may also be taken into account. Apart from these judgements of how others are likely to react, some parole board members may make their decisions on the basis of what they think the 'proper' amount of time an offender should serve for a particular offence, regardless of his readiness for release. Widely publicised cases are most likely to be considered from this perspective.[1]

Many parole board members will claim that some of these considerations do not enter into their decisions. Others would want to expand the list or to make it more specific. The above certainly are not what every parole board member considers in reaching his decision on every case, but all are factors which some board members take into account on some cases.

The National Parole Institutes, an organisation devoted to the study and improvement of parole services in the United States, compiled the results of questionnaires returned by 139 state parole board members, almost half of those in the United States.[2] In these questionnaires the members were asked to set forth their estimate of how often, in the preceding year, they took into

Table 8.1

Considerations in parole decisions

Column A: Estimates by parole board members of the percentage of cases they heard in past year in which various considerations affected 'consciously and significantly' their decisions to grant or deny parole. *Column B*: Designation by these board members of 'the five most important' of these considerations 'for a parole board member', regardless of the frequency with which they were considered.

Considerations	*A*. Median % of cases in which this consideration consciously and significantly influenced their decision	*B*. % of board members including it as one of the five most important considerations
1. My estimate of the chances that the prisoner would or would not commit a serious crime if paroled.	79.4	92.8
2. My judgement that the prisoner would become a worse risk if confined longer.	13.6	71.9
3. My judgement that the prisoner would benefit from further experience in the institution programme, or at any rate, would become a better risk if confined longer.	27.6	87.1
4. My judgement that the prisoner had already been punished enough to 'pay' for his crime.	13.3	43.2
5. What I thought the reaction of the local police might be if the prisoner were granted parole.	3.0	12.2
6. What I thought the reaction the press, radio and TV might be if the prisoner were granted parole.	3.5	8.6
7. What I thought the reaction of the judge might be if the prisoner were granted parole.	7.5	20.9

Considerations	*A.* Median % of cases in which this consideration consciously and significantly influenced their decision	*B.* % of board members including it as one of the five most important considerations
8. What I thought the reaction of other prisoners might be to the policy which they might ascribe to me from my decision in a particular case.	3.7	12.2
9. What I thought the reaction of prison officials might be to my decision in a particular case.	3.1	5.0
10. My feelings about how my decision in this case would affect the feelings or welfare of the prisoner's relatives or dependents.	9.2	33.8
11. What I thought the consequences of my decision policy might be in getting legislative support for the parole system's requests.	0*	7.9
12. What I thought the consequences of my decision policy might be for the governor or for other officials in the executive branch of government.	0.4**	8.6
13. What I thought would be the reactions of my colleagues on the parole board.	0***	9.4
14. The probability that the prisoner would be a misdemeanant and a burden to his parole supervisors, even if he did not commit any serious offences on parole.	8.9	35.3

* 61% of the board members said this was not a consideration in any case.
** 49% of the board members said this was not a consideration in any case.
*** 58% of the board members said this was not a consideration in any case.

account various considerations in their decisions to grant or to deny parole. Column A in Table 8.1 gives the median of the figures entered by these board members after each item. The median of 79.4 for the first consideration, for example, means that half the board members entered a percentage higher than 79.4 and half entered a lower percentage for this item. Part B of Column B gives the percentage of parole board members who included the item in their entries after the statement:

> 'In my opinion, the five most important of the above considerations for a parole board member, regardless of the frequency with which they are considered, are numbers —— —— —— —— ——.'

Table 8.1 reveals that, no matter how one designates or tabulates it, the leading preoccupation of most parole board members, in their decisions to grant or to deny parole, was their judgement on whether or not the prisoner was likely to commit a serious crime if paroled. Nevertheless, only 20% said that this entered 100% of their decisions, and only 35% gave estimates of 90% or higher. Conversely, 2% of the board members said that this consideration entered into less than 10% of their decisions. Regardless of frequency, it was considered one of the five most important considerations by 93% of the board members; only 1 out of 139 did not include it in their five most important items.

The second most influential consideration, of all of those tabulated in Table 8.1, was No. 3, the parole board member's judgement that the prisoner would benefit from further experience in the institution, or at any rate, would become a better risk if confined longer. However, half the parole board members applied this faith in the prison to less than 27.6% of their cases. Indeed, an opposite consideration was third in frequency of use; this is No. 2, the judgement that the prisoner would become a worse risk if confined longer.

No other consideration came close to the first three on the list in the proportion of cases to which they are applied by parole board members, according to their estimates. Thus, while a variety of considerations are bound up in the decision to parole a given individual, and at times these may have little to do with the risk he presents, in the great majority of cases it is the probability of failure on parole that is of most concern to the parole board member.

In his assessment of risk the parole board member may look to a variety of sources depending on his own experiences, education and beliefs. And as we shall see subsequently he may at times err seriously in his estimations. For example, during training sessions with parole board members when the same case history was presented to those in attendance, it was not at all unusual to have estimates varying from 25% to 75% as to the probability that the same offender would succeed on parole.[3] The most substantial errors were usually committed by parole board members who had had little opportunity for systematic feedback on the results of their decisions or had not been exposed to research findings which were available.

Basically there are three sources of data, of varying degrees of completeness and accuracy, which are available to a parole board member at the time of parole consideration: the offender's history prior to incarceration, his activities in prison and the conditions under which he is likely to be released. We shall briefly examine some of the things we know about each of these sources. Subsequently, we shall discuss various techniques of case decision-making. It will be abundantly clear that despite all the information we may gather about parolees in general, predicting how a specific offender will do on parole is a difficult enterprise. It is, at least, less hazardous if one separates facts from fancy when weighing what the available information means.

Pre-incarceration characteristics[4]

The first information available on prisoners is that which generally can be learned quickly, such as: sex, race, age, offence, and prior criminal record. Some of these attributes, for example, the offence and criminal record, may actually have intricate variations. However, we shall first consider them as broad categories into which inmates may be classified soon after they reach the prison. We are concerned with the parole prognosis value of this information by which prisoners may be divided into the young and old, the thieves and the murderers, the first offenders and the repeaters, and so forth.

Age at release

One of the most firmly established pieces of statistical knowledge about criminals is that the older a man is when he is released from prison, the less likely he is to return to crime. By no means should it be inferred that all old prisoners are good risks or all youngsters poor risks. Nevertheless, as Table 8.2 shows, for all parolees taken collectively, the older they are at release the less likely they are to fail on parole.

Although there is usually some deviation from perfect consistency, such findings have been reported for many decades, and in numerous jurisdictions. A related finding is that as age at release increases it is increasingly likely that if any further criminality occurs, it will be a misdemeanour rather than a felony.[5]

Table 8.2

Age at release and parole performance, based on one year follow-up of men and women paroled by 22 agencies, January through December, 1965

	PAROLE PERFORMANCE			
Age of release	Number favourable (no major difficulty)	Number unfavourable (major difficulty)	% unfavourable	Total number
21 and under	1,685	736	30.4	2,421
22 – 30	2,220	939	29.7	3,159
31 – 39	1,048	411	28.2	1,459
40 – 51	580	216	27.1	796
52 and over	232	37	13.8	269
Total	5,765	2,339	28.8	8,104

Source: *Uniform Parole Reports*, National Council on Crime and Delinquency, 1967.

The easiest interpretation of this finding is that people become less criminal as they become more mature. Such an interpretation only has much validity if the word 'mature' is used primarily in a non-biological sense. Criminals generally are at least as well developed physically as the average person of their age. They can only be considered immature by defining normal maturation as change from a delinquent youth to a non-criminal adulthood.

It will suffice at this point to observe that the age group which has the highest crime rates in most industrialised societies is the vaguely defined one which is in transition between childhood and adulthood – the people we call 'adolescents'. For them to become adults, in the sense that others treat them as adults, requires not just physical maturation, but the acquisition of a self-sufficient position in the adult economic and social world. Prisoners tend to be persons who have failed in the past and may be handicapped in the future in achieving this transition, although most of them eventually do become self-sufficient in a legitimate adult life.

Duration and extent of prior criminality

The duration of prior criminality can be estimated imperfectly from several types of evidence. For example, offenders can be differentiated according to the age at which they were first arrested, first adjudicated, first committed to a correctional institution, or first reported in any type of difficulty for delinquent activity. Presumably, among offenders of approximately the same age, the earlier they first have any of these experiences, the longer is the span of their prior involvement in crime, and the more likely they are to continue in crime. This is indicated by Table 8.3.

The foregoing conclusion has occasionally been challenged by a theory that all offenders have approximately the same period of delinquency and crime to go through, so that the earlier they start this period, the younger they will be when they conclude it. This is suggested by the finding that many older chronic offenders have no juvenile delinquency or youth crime record.[6]

Nevertheless, the predominance of evidence is against this conclusion. Despite some deviations, the overall generalisation indicated by Table 8.3 is that at any age, the longer the span of prior criminality, the more likely it is that it will be extended in the future. Unfortunately, not many cross tabulations of violation rates are available which relate age at release to age of first arrest as does Table 8.3.

Another measure relating prior criminal behaviour to parole

outcome is shown in Table 8.4. These tabulations indicate, on the whole, that the overall trend is for the parole failure rate to increase as the magnitude of this prior experience increases. However, a few rather persistent types of crime characteristically starting at a later age, provide exceptions to the foregoing generalisation that early onset or serious prior records means more persistence in crime. These late starting offences consist of some crimes associated with alcoholism, especially cheque forgery, and some offences that also seem to occur as an abnormal adjustment to senility. These include a theft and vagrancy combination, and certain sexual indecency offences. The old and persistent criminals who do not have a criminal record which goes back to juvenile days, or have a long gap between youth and old age offences, are not sufficiently numerous to contradict the overall generalisation that the younger a person was when his crime began, the more likely he is to persist in it.

Table 8.3

Post-release failure rates of US Federal adult male prisoners according to age at release and age at first arrest (number of cases indicated in parentheses)

Age at first arrest	All Cases	*Age at release from prison* 18–21	22–25	26–35	36 and over
16 and under	46% (304)	53% (94)	43% (68)	43% (106)	40% (35)
17 – 20	38% (316)	37% (49)	45% (73)	41% (116)	28% (78)
21 and over	24% (395)	–	24% (37)	24% (184)	24% (174)

Source: *U.S. Federal Prison and Parole Study, 1964**.

* A study directed by Daniel Glaser, the results of which are reported in his book *The Effectiveness of a Prison and Parole System*, Indianapolis, 1964.

Table 8.4

Number of prior commitments to adult correctional institutions and parole performance, based on one year follow-up of males paroled by 55 agencies, January through December, 1968

Number of prior prison commitments	Number favourable (no major difficulty)	Number unfavourable (major difficulty)	Per cent unfavourable	Total number
None	11,333	3,827	25%	15,160
One	3,058	1,520	33%	4,578
Two	1,359	723	35%	2,082
Three	616	372	38%	988
Four of more	516	422	45%	938
Total	16,882	6,864	29%	23,746

Source: Uniform Parole Reports, National Council on Crime and Delinquency, 1970.

Types of offence

Still another aspect of the vital information provided to parole boards by the criminal record is the type of offence for which a prisoner is currently committed, or in which he was previously involved. The most persistent types of common crime are those in which offenders obtain someone else's money without use of violence. These crimes can be divided into two major categories: illegal service and predatory crimes.

Illegal service crimes consist of economically motivated offences in which there is no person who clearly considers himself a victim; instead, the persons with whom the criminals deal are his customers. Examples of such crimes are the sale of stolen goods, and the provision of illegal gambling and prostitution services. Only a minute proportion of these offences lead to arrest and prosecution. Also, conviction on some of these charges, such as gambling and prostitution, seldom leads to imprisonment, so parole boards seldom confront such criminals. Because these criminal services are both more profitable and safer than most other offences, one can reasonably speculate that they may be the most frequently committed clearly criminal acts, even though this is not confirmed by complaint or arrest statistics.

The crimes usually encountered by parole boards are predatory crimes. As indicated in Table 8.5 on the whole, these offences

Table 8.5

Post-release violation rates in relation to offence, based on one year follow-up of males paroled by 55 agencies, January through December, 1967

Highest violations	*Unfavourable outcome*	*Number of cases*
Vehicle theft	42%	1,069
Theft or larceny	33%	1,872
Burglary	33%	6,123
Forgery fraud	38%	2,140
Intermediate and inconsistent		
Armed robbery	27%	2,373
Narcotics drug laws	30%	970
Lowest violations		
Forcible rape	19%	459
Aggravated assault	23%	1,144
Wilful homicide	12%	1,504

Source: Uniform Parole Reports, National Council on Crime and Delinquency, 1969.

usually fall into three main clusters, from the standpoint of violation rates. The offences usually associated with the highest violation rates involve taking somebody else's property by stealth or by deceit. Notable here are the crimes of theft, burglary and forgery.

Theft or larceny, consists simply of taking somebody else's property. Both in the law and in statistical tabulations, the crime of auto theft is usually treated separately. Auto thieves have the highest rates of parole violation in most jurisdictions, possibly because they generally are the youngest parolees. Their crime usually is commited for the temporary enjoyment of transportation rather than for long-term economic gains. For this reason, in a very high percentage of auto thefts the vehicle is recovered intact, even though the thieves usually are not caught. However, in some auto thefts the cars are stripped, and some older auto thieves are in gangs who falsify ownership papers and sell stolen cars.

Other types of theft include shoplifting, removing objects from parked cars, picking pockets, taking goods from places of employment, and many more varieties of 'stealing'. Most of the separate crimes are small, frequently they are not immediately discovered by the victim, and probably a major portion are never reported to the police. Only a small proportion of theft reported to the police, other than auto theft, is solved by recovery of the stolen goods, or conviction of the offenders. Furthermore, the small value of the property taken in separate offences frequently results in a convicted person receiving only a minor penalty, so that most of the time they never get to prison or receive only a short sentence.

Burglary consists of breaking and entering for the purpose of committing a felonious act, and it sometimes is designated as 'breaking' or 'breaking and entering'. Usually it is committed in conjunction with larceny at the place entered. However, burglary almost always carries a more severe penalty than larceny alone, so the offenders usually are prosecuted only for burglary. Some laws make 'burglary and larceny' a single compound offence. A majority of persons arrested for burglary in the United States are under 19 years of age, but an appreciable number of burglars who are encountered in prison populations are older. These often include those for whom burglary has become a profession in which they work closely with dealers of stolen goods ('fences').

Another kind of recurrent economic offence not involving violence is the crime of forgery. Forgers differ from most criminals in the extent to which they commit their crimes alone, and in being relatively older. Petty or naïve forgery is notably associated with chronic alcoholism. Perhaps because cashing a fraudulent cheque requires a certain amount of facility at writing, and an appearance of success, forgers are also distinctive in generally having more education and less often coming from an impoverished home than most prisoners. Other types of fraud, often called 'confidence games' are less often associated with alcoholism than simple cheque forgery, and are more frequently persistent criminal professions. Embezzlement is a special kind of fraud, frequently involving violation of trust by a prominent and presumably trustworthy citizen, so that he is placed in a government or business position where he handles much money. These offenders generally are good risk as far as prospects for violation are concerned, but their parole poses special public relations problems.

The selling of narcotics has already been mentioned as an illegal service crime. Other narcotic offences include illegal possession, use, and purchase of narcotic drugs. Evidence on the relative risk of these narcotic offenders as parolees is inconsistent. There is some indication that they have very high violation rates when they are paroled to neighbourhoods where narcotics usage is extensive, but that they have average or below average violation rates elsewhere.

Robbery is different from the economically motivated crimes described earlier, in that robbery involves the use or threat of violence in order to procure someone else's property. Like narcotics offences, it is associated with diverse violation or recidivism rates in different jurisdictions, but robbers generally seem to have about the average violation rate for their age group. However, they are of concern to parole boards because of the serious injury or death which they may cause. Robbers vary tremendously in character. They include groups of adolescents in slum areas who 'roll' drunks coming from taverns in the late hours of night, naïve individuals who make a foolhardy effort to solve economic crises by trying to hold up a large bank (often without a working weapon), and some highly dangerous individuals who have a psychological drive to hurt their victims.

The cluster of offences associated with the lowest violation rates on parole are crimes which least often serve as vocations. These include homicide and rape. However, the strong public demand for punishment as an expression of revenge against such offenders, plus the extreme importance of preventing recurrence of these crimes, makes parole boards exceptionally cautious in paroling those who commit these offences.

Thus far we have dealt only with gross violation rates, although it has been noted that the nature of the probable parole violation may be a crucial consideration in parole decisions. The type of violation likely to be committed, if any, is especially in the forefront of a parole board member's thoughts when he considers the type of offence for which a prisoner was last convicted. William L. Jacks, statistician of The Pennsylvania Board of

Parole, has made one of the few studies of type of violation in relation to type of offence. This is summarised in Table 8.6.

Table 8.6

Type of offence for which committed as a factor in type of offence, if any, committed on parole (for Pennsylvania only)

Offence for which imprisoned	All parolees, 1946–1961* Per cent committing new crimes on parole	Per cent repeating on parole the crime for which imprisoned
Auto larceny	(included in larceny here)	
Larceny	22.5%	6.4%
Burglary	23.4%	11.1%
Forgery	22.3%	10.2%
Robbery	19.5%	5.1%
Narcotics	15.9%	10.1%
Sex offenders	8.8%	2.9%
Assault and battery	12.3%	3.6%
Homicide	5.7%	0.4%
Other offences	10.2%	3.1%
Rates for all cases	18.4%	6.8%
No. of cases	29,346	29,346

* Source: Pennsylvania Board of Parole, 'A Comparison of Releases and Recidivists from June 1, 1946 to May 31, 1961', Harrisburg, Dec. 20, 1961.

This table indicates first, that in the State of Pennsylvania the offences fell into three main clusters in terms of prospects of committing a new crime on parole, and these clusters were much like those for overall violation rates shown in Table 8.5. However, larceny and narcotics offences are ranked somewhat differently in these two compilations. Burglars, forgers, and narcotic drug offenders were most likely to commit the same offences, while larceny and robbery were an intermediate cluster, followed by felonious assault and sex offenders. Homicides were lowest, only about one in 250 committed a homicide on parole after being imprisoned for homicide. The gravity of this offence, of course, still makes any repetition a crucial concern.

Other gross traits

Among the other gross traits by which offenders can be rather easily and reliably classified at the time of admission to prison, few have demonstrated a consistent relationship to parole violation. For example, since the 19th century there was much effort to explain crime as the expression of an inherited characteristic that could be identified by a person's physical appearance. One still frequently hears people say that somebody looks like a criminal, or that someone else looks like he could not possibly be a criminal. However, parole board members often observe a fine appearance in some individuals who have shocking criminal records.

There have been popular experiments to investigate the ability to predict criminality from physical appearance. The most useless efforts involved asking people to judge character from photographs of criminals mixed with photographs of highly respected non-criminal persons, when all persons portrayed were of about the same age and wore similar apparel. These studies demonstrated almost complete failure of this approach to character judgement.

Years ago a study found that height and weight had no relationship to parole violation.[7] Classification of people by their general physical condition has not uncovered clear and consistent findings of marked deviation from average violation rates. Some studies find those in poor health or having a handicap have slightly higher than average violation rates, while others found these individuals slightly more successful on parole than the average.

Sex differences are equally poor predictors of parole performance. Males coming before parole boards in most jurisdictions outnumber females in a ratio of about twenty to one. This probably occurs both because females in our society commit felonies less often than males do, and because those females who are convicted of felonies are less likely to receive a sentence of imprisonment than are males. Table 8.7 shows that female parolees violate parole at almost precisely the same rates as males.

Table 8.7

Parole outcome by sex based on one year follow-up of those paroled by 55 agencies, January through December, 1968

Sex	Number	Unfavourable number	Outcome per cent
Male	24,786	7,115	29%
Female	1,720	474	29%

Source: Uniform Parole Reports, National Council on Crime and Delinquency, 1970.

Information about an offender's intelligence is also usually available to a parole board since intelligence tests are almost invariably administered to the inmates of correctional institutions today. They are used to determine the appropriate education, work, and treatment of each prisoner. Despite the convenient availability of this information, it has been found to have only a slight relationship to parole outcome. There is little consistent pattern of violation rate according to intelligence. Generally the most mentally deficient inmates do not do as well on parole as most prisoners, but usually their violation rates are not extremely different from those of many with above average intelligence scores.

A prisoner's intelligence test score, of course, can reflect his capacity for both legal and illegal types of behaviour. It may be significant information for the parole board as an indication of whether an expected parole job is within a parolee's capacity. It may also be the basis for speculation that certain inmates would be particularly dangerous if they returned to crime. However, it is surprising how often crimes reflect emotional behaviour not guided by much intelligent thinking, even when the offender has considerable mental capacity.

An additional consideration to be kept in mind is that intelligence tests are never perfectly accurate, and those given in a prison or other correctional institutions are often exceptionally unreliable. Although the test scores theoretically reflect on inherited mental capacity, it is well known that performance on many of these tests is greatly affected by exposure to schooling, by the type of vocabulary which an individual needed in his social environment, by experience in using the type of arithmetic and mathematics included in the test, and especially, by motivation to perform well. These tests often under-rate a prison inmate's intelligence because he is indifferent or hostile about taking the test at the time it is administered, usually when he is new to the prison, and because he has not been involved in school for some time. Frequently, the scores on these tests increase if they are administered again after the inmates have attended a prison school for an extended period. It should also be noted that intelligence scores sometimes are erroneously high in correctional institutions because of lax control in administering the tests or in recording their results.

Race is also a poor indicator of likely poor outcome. For example, although Negroes in the United States have a higher rate of arrest, conviction, and imprisonment for crimes than whites, most tabulations show little marked or consistent difference in the parole violation rates of the two groups. It is probable that the higher crime rates among Negroes occur largely because they, more often than whites, experience conditions associated with high crime rates in all racial groups. These conditions include low income, high unemployment, low level of education, and residence in slum areas which have long had high crime rates.

These conditions conducive to high crime rates usually are also associated with high parole violation rates. The fact that Negro parole violation rates are not consistently higher than those of whites, therefore, is somewhat puzzling. It may reflect more careful selection of Negroes for parole than of whites, or more frequent institutionalisation of unadvanced offenders among negroes than among whites. There is some evidence that the latter occurs with juvenile delinquents, but evidence as to its occurrence in prison is conflicting.[8]

The differences in crime or parole violation rates for various ethnic groups could readily develop as a consequence of police or parole officers not treating every person in the same fashion for a given type of behaviour, regardless of the person's ethnic descent. Statistics to assess whether or not this occurs are not available on a widespread and recent basis. A common impression is that officials tend to overlook infractions committed by minority group members in their own community, and to be unusually severe in dealing with infractions which members of minorities commit elsewhere. This, of course, could be conducive to habituation of minority group members to criminal behaviour, which they might engage in wherever they encounter an opportunity.

Japanese and Chinese are infrequent in correctional institution populations. In California, where they are most numerous, they have a lower violation rate than other parolees. This probably reflects the close-knit community and family support which they receive.

In general, the evidence on race as a factor in the evaluation of parolees suggests that it is not of much predictive utility in itself. However, an understanding of the different social and cultural worlds from which members of some minorities come, and to which they return, may be useful in understanding their offences and in evaluating their parole plans.

There are some personal characteristics which do show a statistical relationship with parole outcome, but they are of limited usefulness in estimating the probability that a specific groups of inmates will succeed or fail on parole. The information discussed earlier – age at release, prior criminal record and present offence – represent the most useful data for that purpose. Very few pieces of information increase the likelihood that one will be greatly aided in forecasting how a group of inmates will do on parole, once the effect of these three pieces of information are taken into account.

But despite this limitation other types of information must be and are sought by parole board members. To begin with, they are concerned by and large with individual not group decisions. They want to know how *this* particular inmate will behave on parole if released now. As we shall see later, the kind of group information we have been discussing here is only marginally useful for that kind of decision.

Secondly, information as age or prior record, is not subject to change. And it is precisely this kind of information which is crucial to a parole board member. In practical fact, a parole decision rarely involves the question whether someone should or should not be released from prison. The question in the overwhelming majority of cases is not *if* but *when* an inmate should be released and under what conditions. For this kind of decision, information which can show changes or varies in some fashion over time is critical. It is that kind of information which tells us when the chances of success have increased or under what condition parole outcome is likely to be increased in the future.

Now obviously the present and future are much more subject to influence than is the past. Thus information relating to prison adjustment and release plans offer some of the most important sources of information to a parole board member. It is to these we will now turn our attention.

Parole and the prison record

Onc of the major advantages of parole is to defer the decision on how long an offender should be confined. Instead of deciding on the duration of confinement purely from what one can learn at the time of trial, additional time is allowed, in part, to permit further observation of the offender. But what can one learn by watching a man in confinement that permits one to improve one's judgement about the risk in releasing him? Indeed, might one be misled if one relied on behaviour in the unnatural stresses of prison life to predict behaviour under conditions of greater freedom, opportunity and responsibility in the free community? These are difficult questions, and our ability to answer them with accuracy is far from satisfactory. Nevertheless, we have a few facts relevant to this problem, and there is evidence available on the means by which an enterprising correctional system could gather more facts.

Change in parole risks with passage of time

In the National Parole Institutes poll, members of all parole boards in the United States were asked to estimate the per cent of all cases in which the belief that the inmate would become a better risk if confined longer was an important consideration in their decisions on granting or denying him parole. The median estimate of the per cent of all cases in which this was an active influence on their decision was 27.6%. The median estimate of the per cent of parole decisions markedly influenced by a belief that the inmate would become a worse risk if confined longer was 13.6%.

Although we have subjective impressions of change in parole risk with time served, there are no objective statistics which justify simple generalisations on this matter that might be applicable to most cases. As Table 8.8 shows, actual violation rates for most types of offenders increase with time served until some peak is reached, then decline. The difficulty in interpreting figures like these is that they represent two factors: actual change in parole risk with passage of time, and a selective process by the court in sentencing and the parole board in granting parole, whereby those confined longest are presumed to be the worst risks. The fact that those confined the very longest do not have peak violation rates probably is due in large part to the long sentences given homicide and some sex offence cases. As brought out earlier, these generally are not professional criminals and they rarely repeat their crimes after imprisonment, as do those who have made their living by crime. However, public outrage at offenders who commit violent crimes against persons leads to an insistence that less risk be taken with them than with property offenders.

To know with more certainty the relationship of post-release violation rates purely to change during imprisonment one would have to conduct controlled experiments. A parole board would have to take a group of inmates ostensibly similar and divide them by purely random methods, such as by tossing coins, into groups to be confined for different durations of time. If this were done rigorously with a significantly large number of inmates, and if the fact that purely random selection was used were kept secret, we could be confident in concluding that differences in post-release violation rates for those confined for different durations of time would reflect almost exclusively the effects of time confined. Of course, the more we repeated this experiment in different institutions and got similar results, the more confident we would become that duration of confinement was the only significant variable accounting for our findings.

We are quite certain that almost every parole board would

Table 8.8

Parole violation rate in relation to time served before parole

Offender Group	Violation rates according to time served (Time units indicated for each offender group)					Violation rates for all cases (& ? Cases)
Washington State adult parolees	1 yr. or less	13–24 months	25–36 months	37–48 months	Other (as indicated)	
	31%	40%	40%	39%	(49–60 months: 37%)	38% (1,731)
					(61–72 months: 29%) (73–84 months: 29%) (85–96 months: 29%)	
Federal prison releases	Less than one year	1–2 yrs.	2–3 yrs.	3 yrs. and over		
	27%	35%	44%	40%		35% (1,015)

Source: Washington State Board of Prison and Paroles, *Adult Parolee Study, 1960* and *U.S. Federal Prison and Parole Study, 1964*.

consider such an experiment illegal, if not immoral, so it is not likely to occur. Yet something approximating this has been done several times by State of California parole agencies, which have assigned persons to combined early release and intensive supervision programmes by purely random methods, so that their records could be compared to those of a control group confined for the regular release and supervision programme. The main point to be made here is that it is likely more possible to experiment with scientific rigour in release policy, provided the purely random selection is only for earlier than usual release, rather than for longer confinement.

If we cannot conduct a deliberate experiment, we can approximate one somewhat by comparing the post-release records of groups of similar inmates confined for different lengths of time. For example, it has been found that federal prisoners with no record of prior institutional commitment have about the same post-release criminal record regardless of time confined, but the post-release failure rate increases with time confined for federal prisoners with one or more prior institutional commitments. This is indicated in Table 8.9. However, we would have to group inmates by more traits than their prior institutional commitments alone to be confident that we were comparing groups of inmates similar in every important respect except time confined.

Unfortunately, no study has been made of the influence of time served in conjunction with other classifications of inmates by many common characteristics. Such a study would have to be made with a very large number of case records on past releasees, in order to have data on appreciable numbers who appear to have been similar in many important respects. We should, ideally, be able to compare the trends in violation rate with time served for different types of offenders, with types categorised by combinations of age, offence, criminal record, and other crucial variables. Although selective factors determining duration of confinement might still include factors other than those by which the inmates are grouped, these tabulations would suggest quite strongly what experience indicates has been the statistically optimum duration of confinement for each type of offender. Even if this would not be an absolute guide for a parole board in determining when a particular individual should be released, such figures would provide broad principles against

Table 8.9

Per cent post-release failures in relation to time served and prior institutional commitments

Prior institutional commitments	Months served before release: 12 months or less	13 through 24 months	25 through 36 months	37 months or more	All cases
None	21% (125)	25% (137)	28% (40)	16% (31)	23% (333)
One or more	31% (150)	40% (303)	49% (139)	48% (90)	41% (682)
All cases	27% (275)	35% (440)	44% (179)	40% (121)	35% (1,015)

Source: *Federal Prison and Parole Study, 1964.*

which special factors in individual cases might be weighted.

Even more important than knowing the overall relationships between time served and the post-release records of particular categories of inmates, would be knowledge of the specific observations which provide the most reliable signs that an inmate is changing for better or for worse in prison. There are six main types of information on which judgements of change during confinement now are made. These are: disciplinary record; education in prison; participation in counselling, therapy or religious services; performance at prison work; staff impressions on change of attitude; and, evidence of change from the inmate's arrangements and plans in the outside world.

Rule infractions and punishments in prison

Traditionally parole is regarded by the public as a reward for good behaviour in prison. This also is implied by many parole boards, in their public relations statements justifying their decisions in particular cases. However, rewarding or punishing prison conduct seldom is set forth today officially as the major policy guiding parole decisions. Nevertheless, prison conduct often is unofficially taken into account in parole decisions. This is part of the latent function of parole, in contributing to the control of inmates by prison officials. When parole board members were asked to estimate the per cent of their decisions in the previous year in which their granting or denying parole was significantly affected by what they thought the reaction of prison officials would be, 43% said that this consideration never or practically never significantly affected their decision. However, 37% estimated it was a factor in 1 to 9% of their decisions, ten per cent estimated it affected 10 to 19 per cent of their decisions, five per cent said it affected 20 to 29% of their decisions, and the remaining five per cent distributed their estimates from 30 to 89%.

Regardless of these policy variations, research has generally found that this misconduct listed in official disciplinary records of prisoners has only a small relationship to the success or failure of the offenders on parole. This is indicated in Table 8.10. In the two jurisdictions shown, the rate of post-release violations tended to be greater for inmates with records of rule infractions in prison than for those without such records. However, the number of infractions did not provide an extremely discriminating or consistent basis for predicting violation rates. In an Illinois Youthful Male Parolee study a separate tabulation was made for major rather than minor rule infractions, the major infractions being those which could be considered crimes on the outside (theft, assault, fraud, etc.). Also, on the assumption that there might be most prognostic significance in persistence of infractions even after the initial period of adjustment to imprisonment, a separate tabulation was made of parole violation rates in relation to disciplinary infractions during the last third of the period of confinement. However, these provided only a rather slight improvement over prediction by total number of infractions.[9]

A more adequate analysis would consider the differential relationship of prison infractions to parole outcome for different types of offenders. When this was done in the Federal Prison and Parole Study it was found that an unsatisfactory prison adjustment record was not markedly related to recidivism rates for inmates who were serving their first term of institutional confinement, but for those with prior confinement (in jail, training school or prison), those with unsatisfactory prison adjustment had

Table 8.10

Post-release violation rates in relation to prison disciplinary record

Minnesota adult male parolees		
Number of institution misbehaviour 'marks'	Number of cases	Violation rate
None	325	43%
1 or 2	118	54%
3 or more	82	49%
All cases	525	46%

Federal adult male releases		
Progress report comment on conformity to rules	Number of cases	Reimprisonment rate
No infractions reported	695	30%
Infractions considered negligible	85	34%
Infractions noted but none quasi-felonious	97	53%
Infractions include assaults	41	51%
Infractions include serious deception	60	45%
Infractions include assault and serious deception	27	44%
Other quasi-felonious infractions	10	50%
Total cases	1,015	35%

Source: Richard Samelian, *Parole Success and Failure: A Study of the Influence of Selected Socio-Economic and Personal Factors and Their Effect on Parole Outcome*, M.S.W. Thesis, University of Minnesota, 1962, and *Federal Prison and Parole Study, 1964*.

a 58% reimprisonment rate, in contrast with a 38% reimprisonment rate for those with satisfactory prison adjustment. In an analysis of Federal Youth Correction Act cases alone, a prison discplinary record was found to be predictive of high parole violation rates primarily for prisoners with 5th grade or lower educational achievement and no institutional commitments prior to their 16th birthday.

There are probably two major reasons for the frequent smallness of the relationship of the prison disciplinary record to post-release conduct. First, the significance of a misconduct record depends upon the disciplinary practices of the prison. This varies greatly from one institution to the next, and is seldom highly consistent within any prison. The second reason is that a misconduct record has quite different significance for different types of prisoners.

In traditionally strict prisons there are a number of fairly explicit rules, and every infraction of them is recorded and punished. This is discipline 'by the book'. Sometimes these rules are extremely repressive and rather petty, and sometimes they are fairly liberal. All prisons, of course, have rules against behaviour that would be considered felonious on the outside, such as theft, assaults, or sexual immorality. However, prisons vary in the extent to which they try to regulate such things as: talking to another inmate while standing in line, while at work, or at meals; deviating from standard apparel, haircuts, cleanliness, or cell maintenance; being noisy, rude or profane; showing respect for officers.

Some prisons try to prosecute most felonious conduct committed in prison in the public courts in whose jurisdiction the prison is located, particularly where the offence could bring a new sentence greater than that which the inmate already is serving. Other prisons prefer not to take the trouble involved in transporting inmates to court, supplying staff or inmate witnesses, and so forth.

Apart from this variation in the things on which rules are promulgated, prisons differ in whether they have the same penalty for every infraction of a specific rule, or impose disciplinary punishment on an individual basis. Some vary the penalty according to the attitude and behaviour of the offender, rather than making it uniform for specific offences.

A disciplinary record, thus, may reflect the prison, but it also does show something about an individual's ability to adjust to imprisonment. This may or may not be highly indicative of his ability to avoid violation of parole. For example, persons highly committed to crime as a profession frequently have extensive experience in prison, and are adept at 'getting along' there. Many wardens find that the 'old-time convicts' make the best prisoners, since they know what is expected of them in prison. Conversely, some prisoners highly committed to a law-abiding life may be especially upset by imprisonment, and they may be pressured by the more criminalistic inmates in a manner which impairs ability to conform to prison staff expectations. Thus a record of fighting in prison may show either aggressiveness, emotional instability, social ineptness, or defensive efforts of a prisoner to avoid subordination to more aggressive inmates.

Parole boards frequently are expected to collaborate with prison officials in maintaining custodial control over a prison by using the granting or denial of parole as a reward or penalty, respectively, for inmate conformity to prison rules. If prison conduct becomes the major factor in parole decisions, the functions of parole other than regulating conduct in prison will be sacrificed. Also, the effective penalties for prison misconduct may often involve the imposition of long added prison terms by parole denial, for petty misdemeanours in prison not tried by proper judicial processes. Most boards pursue a policy of regarding prison conduct as just one of many considerations entering into their separate assessments of parole prospects in each individual case.

Unusually serious misconduct in prison at the time of the hearing or the release date frequently is made a basis for an automatic but brief delay in a parole hearing, or in the issuance of parole release orders. Often this linkage of parole with minimal conformity to prison rules is explicitly stated and followed as board policy, as a contribution to the support of prison staff authorities. This is different from making parole highly dependent on a clear disciplinary record. If this delay of hearing or release is not done with some flexibility and closely checked, petty difficulties in prison can result in serious jeopardy to promising parole prospects.

Education in prison

Parole and emphasis on education in prison began almost simultaneously, in that they were both identified with the beginnings of the Reformatory Movement at Elmira in New York State in 1876. Under that institution's 'mark' system, points towards the earning of parole were awarded to inmates on the basis of their completion of education courses, including both academic and vocational training programmes. This use of parole to motivate positive efforts at self-improvement in prison, rather than just to motivate avoidance of penalties for misconduct, has been a fairly consistent characteristic of parole practice everywhere.

Despite this, there is considerable evidence that the hope of impressing the parole board favourably is a major factor in motivating inmates in education courses in prison. A survey of inmate opinion in five federal prisons in the United States indicated clearly that most prisoners were convinced that improving one's education while in prison increased one's chances for parole. Nevertheless, the same study, when endeavouring to determine the relationship between educational progress in prison and success on parole, did not find a clear relationship in these federal prisons. The inmates who were in prison school programmes did not, on the whole, succeed on parole more often than did those who were not in the prison education programme. This is inconsistent with findings in several studies in state prisons which found somewhat more association between participating in prison education and succeeding on parole.[10]

It is evident that the significance of a prison education for parole outcome is not a simple matter. It may often be the case that inmates who are most retarded in education because of their school adjustment before prison are the ones most often required to attend school in prison. Under these circumstances of involuntary participation in prison education, one would expect the students to be worse parole risks than other inmates not because of their assignment to prison school, but because of their prior long-run antipathy to schooling. Conversely, in prisons where attendance in school is a highly voluntary matter, only the most conventionally oriented inmates may be educated there. Their better records on parole may thus reflect attitudes that distinguished them from other prisoners initially, apart from whatever additional improvement in their parole prospects may have resulted from their schooling.

In addition to determining who is assigned to prison school and how, if the parole board is to evaluate the significance of prison school records, it should determine what alternative programmes are available for the inmate in prison. It may be that assignment to school is an alternative to assignment in a prison industry or maintenance job where work skills and habits would be acquired that might be more significant in post-release employment than the small amount of schooling which can be acquired in the limited time in prison. Of course, the education which an inmate procures in prison may be a voluntary effort, pursued in spare time, in addition to a full day's performance at a work assignment. Presumably this would make it especially significant as a favourable parole predictor. In short, one cannot evaluate prison records well unless one is highly familiar with the educational and vocational training programmes and schedules available for inmates at a specific institution.

One serious deficiency in some prison education is its tendency to create occupational aspirations in inmates far beyond their vocational qualifications, and beyond any qualifications which a prison school provides. Frequently inmates whose educational achievement is well below the high school level express hopes of employment in highly technical or professional occupations requiring much more education than they are likely ever to get, and certainly more than they would be qualified for for many years after release from prison even if they could pursue the life of a full-time student. Frequently inmates learn a skill in prison that is primarily an avocation, such as playing a musical instrument, and their sole ambition is to be employed in this activity. While instances of professional musicians, athletes or artists beginning in prison have been reported, they certainly are extremely rare. Unless there is evidence of definite recognition of this talent by outside persons who clearly can provide wholesome post-release sponsorship, occupational aspirations of this sort, based almost entirely on prison training, probably can be considered as indicative of a prospective frustrating experience for the parolee.

Despite all of the foregoing, the overall picture from statistical studies is that an inmate who has a long record of persistent educational pursuit in prison, a person who has distinctly raised his grade record, or a person who has acquired a diploma while in prison, is likely to be a significantly better parole risk than someone who does not have this educational achievement record. Education is not enough to substitute for other types of rehabilitation for most criminals, but education can be a major asset and support in conjunction with other changes. In addition, new experiments in programmed education promise much more dramatic benefits from prison education in the future than have been demonstrated heretofore. The Draper Youth Prison at Draper, Alabama has yielded preliminary reports of marked reduction in recidivism following dramatic educational and social relationship status change through special inmate mutual and self-teaching programmes based on psychological reinforcement theory.

Counselling, therapy and religious programmes in prison

Inmates in many prisons are able presently to participate in group counselling and group psychotherapy. The latter term generally is used for groups led by psychiatrists, psychologists or psychiatric social workers, but counselling groups have been organised by a large proportion of the custodial, administrative and treatment staff in several prison systems. Fortunately, we have the benefit of extensive comparisons of the post-release records of inmates in counselling and therapy groups in California, compared to the records of inmates not in these groups. In some of their studies the inmates were randomly assigned to group programmes, to assure their comparability, as a whole, with those not in such programmes. The predominant finding, again and again, is that those in these groups do not have appreciably better or worse post-release criminal records than those not in groups. The only clear exception is that inmates long in groups with the same staff leader, on the whole, have less further criminality than those briefly in groups, in groups with turnover of staff leadership, or not in groups.[11] This suggests that it is the personal relationship which develops with the staff member who is the group leader that is the most rehabilitative influence in these group programmes.

It should also be noted that other correctional benefits than reduction of post-release crime may result from group programmes; they seem to improve the inmate's adjustment to imprisonment, including his rapport with both staff and other inmates, through providing a means of ventilating discontent, analysing its sources, and perhaps rectifying them. They give the inmate a 'vocabulary of adjustment', so that he is likely to be enhanced in his ability to convey to staff, parole board members and others the impression that he has gained insight into the causes of his criminality. By the hard criterion of post-release criminality, this ostensible insight into causes of his own crime does not seem to be a dependable sign of ability to overcome the causes, even assuming that the causes are identified accurately.

Although California research on group counselling and group

therapy has included studies of many variations of intensity in these programmes as measured in hours per day or per week, and has included sophisticated analyses of differences according to type of prisoner and type of institution, there is no analysis by style of group leadership. Conversations with California therapists and visits to their group sessions reveal much variation in the extent to which their group discussions are staff rather than inmate directed (or in the latter case, allegedly non-directed), and in the focus of this direction. It still is possible that some group styles reduce criminality in some inmates, while the same or other styles enhance criminality in other inmates; research which makes more relevant distinctions might reveal this, thus providing a basis for better prison and parole policy.

Controlled experiments for the evaluation of individual therapy in prison, as a source of reduction in recidivism, have had mixed results. In the California Youth Authority's Nelles School for Boys and its Preston School of Industry, in 1959 and 1960, inmates referred to a psychiatric team (psychiatrist, psychologists and psychiatric social workers) and accepted as amenable to treatments by them were randomly divided into experimental and control groups, with only the former receiving services from these teams. As of 15 months after release from the institution, the Preston experimentals had a significantly higher violation rate than their controls, while the reverse was true at Nelles, especially for the more serious offenders there. The Nelles boys had a median age of 15.1 and the Preston boys 17.5. There was only one psychiatrist at each institution.[12] Was it the older age and the longer delinquency career of the Preston boys, or was it the qualities of the individual psychiatrists and their teams, that account for the opposite results of these two experiments?

More dramatic and clear-cut benefits from individual counselling were reported from the Pilot Intensive Counselling Organisation, or 'PICO' project at California's Devel Vocational Institution, but not for all types of offender. Over 1600 youths between 1955 and 1961 were classified by clinical judgement as 'amenable' or 'non-amenable' to treatment, the amenables being more expressive of a desire for psychological help, more anxious and/or more intelligent than the non-amenables. Each of these groups was randomly divided into an experimental and a control group, with the former receiving individual therapy, mainly by psychiatric social workers, each of whom had caseloads of only 25. As of thirty-three months after release, the amenable experimental group had an average of almost three months less reconfinement than the amenable controls, but the non-amenable experimental group averaged somewhat more reconfinement than the non-amenable controls.[13]

Much other counselling and therapy has occurred in correctional institutions, on a individual and group basis, but hardly any of it has been evaluated in terms of post-release implications as rigorously as were these programmes. The United States Army Disciplinary Barracks at Fort Leavenworth, Kansas developed a programme which it calls 'One to One Counselling by Custodially Oriented Personnel'. This has impressively improved prison adjustment, partly by helping the inmates to solve problems of their outside relationships which were disturbing them, but it has neither been experimentally administered nor measured in terms of post-release consequences.

There is a variety of evidence that some types of therapy and counselling help some inmates, but a deficiency of demonstrably valid generalisations on what types help what kinds of inmates. In the absence of such knowledge, a parole board can only seek the most rigorous testing possible for each treatment programme, and evaluate the reports of counsellors and therapists on an individual case basis. This becomes part of the general problem of evaluating case assessments by prison staff, which is discussed later in this chapter.

Every prison in the United States has some sort of religious service available to inmates. This ranges from Sunday church services by part-time chaplains recruited from the local ministry, to religious education classes, clubs, pastoral counselling and diverse religious services, by specially trained full-time chaplains. As with Alcoholics Anonymous and education programmes, much participation in prison religious activity may be motivated by an interest in favourably impressing the parole board, or by the diversion it provides from other prison routines. In general, detailed case reports by the chaplain are desirable, with indication of the prisoner's probable post-release involvement with religious groups – considered in the light of his pre-prison involvement – and its possible bearing on his post-release behaviour. Certainly this should prove much more valuable in assessing parole prospects than reports on mere attendance at prison chapel services or membership in religious organisations. Thus far there has been no rigorous research that we know of on statistical relationships between religious activity in prison and parole prospects.

Prison work performance

Prisons began as workhouses for misdemeants who were classified as 'sturdy beggars' and 'idlers' in the sixteenth century. In the 19th century, when the penalty of confinement largely replaced corporal and capital punishment, an additional penalty of 'hard labour' frequently was added to the sentence of confinement. Much imprisonment imposed extremely severe work, as inmates were used in chain gangs for public construction and were even contracted out to work for private employers who paid the state for the services of the prisoners. In the first quarter of the 20th century prison industries were highly developed, so that after World War I a major portion of United States production of blue denim work clothes and of wooden chairs were made in prison.

The imposition of hard labour in prison largely disappeared in the United States during the Great Depression. Businesses which had to compete with prison-made goods, and labour organisations whose members were unemployed while inmates worked, combined to promote laws greatly curtailing the employment permitted to prisoners. Since the 1930s prison labour has been largely limited to maintenance and food cultivation tasks, plus manufacture of goods for use by state agencies. The only major exception in the United States to this state use pattern is some extensive farming operations in southern prisons which produce crops sold on the open market. In many states prisoners also work on public works remote from population centres, especially at forestry camps. In a few states prisoners are employed for road maintenance.

Within prisons, the intensity of the work is low compared with that found in private employment. One major reason for this is simply the lack of sufficient work, since state-use prison industries are limited in scope. This is partly due to the small market which most states provide for prison products, and because spokesmen for private business interests frequently manage to interfere with the state's procurement from prisons of even those products which prison industries can manufacture.

An additional factor limiting the volume and intensity of prison work is the need to have close custodial supervision of inmates. For this reason most staff-organised inmate activity, not only work but also such things as feeding, distribution of laundry, medical care, and staff interviews, are all handled only during the main shift of prison employees in the central work day. This means that prisoners are available for work as little as five or six hours a day.

The final and perhaps most important limitation on the intensity of inmate work is the inadequacy of motivations and incentives for inmate labour in most prison systems. Many prisons provide little or no special reward or pay for diligent work performance. Even where there are some rewards, they often are distributed in a fairly mechanical fashion, at a uniform rate to inmates with a large range of diligence, so that there is little prospect of an inmate gaining significant extra reward by his work. Indeed, it is often surprising how hard many prisoners work when there is so little tangible reward. The positive personal appreciation and other types of psychological recognition which the staff can provide frequently is the major incentive. An additional factor is the prospect that the staff will favourably report an inmate's work record to the parole board.

It should be noted that most inmates have a very poor pre-prison work record. Since almost 90% of felony crime involves the taking of someone else's money or property, their crimes might be considered an alternative to work. However, it should also be noted that prisoners come disproportionately from those segments of the United States population which have the highest unemployment rates. These are youths who have not completed high school, and especially such youth who also are members of minority groups. Thus the prison begins with a work force most of whom have seldom done vigorous work for an extended and regular period.

Follow-up inquiries with released prisoners indicate that no more than a fifth utilise their prison training in their post-release employment, although this fifth has above average rates of success on parole. What seems to be especially significant is the acquisition of a clear competence in a skilled trade. In general, long assignment at a skilled trade job in prison appears to be distinctly associated with success. The difficulty with all of these types of generalisation is that research has not been adequate to determine conclusively the extent to which post-release success is a function of the selection of particular kinds of inmates for particular jobs in the institution, or is an effect of the job itself.

There is some evidence that the assignment of inmates purely to white collar clerical-type jobs is associated with above average degrees of post-release failure. There is considerable reason to believe that inmates without such qualification for white collar jobs who obtain clerical 'front office' jobs in prison are the 'politician' type who are highly committed to a life of connivance, in and out of prison. They know how to get the best jobs in prison in terms of being close to officials and having a high degree of autonomy in office work. At the same time this interferes with their procurement of more practical work experience and training in prison, which might facilitate their self-sufficiency in the free world. Some of these individuals eventually prove successful in finding legal ways of utilising their skills in personal relations, especially if they obtain sales employment. This, however, is not very frequently available as an immediate post-release job, except for types of selling which are of very uncertain income.

One of the problems in assessing work in prison is the poor quality of information in the files and reports on inmate behaviour and work. Unfortunately, while most of the reporting of an inmate's adjustment in prison is prepared by case workers, the most extensive observations of prisoners are made by the prison work supervision staff. There is considerable evidence that the work supervisors have the greatest impact on inmates, since they are with them on a day-to-day basis, and they are often in a close and co-operative personal relationship. Sometimes work supervising staff are asked to submit regular reports on the inmates under them, but these reports are in terms of vague adjectives, in which the vast majority of inmates are rated indiscriminately as 'superior' or 'excellent'. One major impact which a parole board can have on the quality of prison administration, and on the diagnostic services which observation in prison can yield, is to insist that the prison provide the most meaningful possible work assessment reports, reflecting the impressions of the work supervision staff in consultation with caseworkers and others. Information of the following kind is minimally required.

1. A brief description of the type of work an inmate has been doing; not just the name of the shop or building where he does the work.
2. An evaluation of an inmate's *skill* at this type of work in terms of specific comparison with persons employed at this type of work on the outside; thus the inmate could be rated as outstanding, satisfactory or unsatisfactory for employment at this type of work *outside of prison.*
3. An evaluation of the diligence and the attitudes shown by an inmate at work in prison; what these show as to his probable orientation towards outside work, as well as whether his work speed and workshop behaviour meet outside employment standards.
4. An inmate's past and prospective future improvement in skill and in other requirements for outside employment.

If nothing else, the preparation of such reports might promote in prison staff more attention to the practical value or deficiency of various prison jobs.

Prison staff assessments of inmate attitudes

Most inmates appearing before a parole board obviously have had more personal contact with some members of the prison staff than with others. Frequently the work supervisors of a prison spent five or six days a week, six to eight hours each day, in a small space with as few as five or six inmates. Officers supervising prison housing and recreational units may see the same group of a few dozen prisoners every day. Even when they supervise large numbers of inmates, so that they do not develop much familiarity with most of them, a few inmates become well known to them.

These people frequently have the opportunity to hear the inmate when he is speaking less guardedly about his past or his future than he is likely to speak in the formal situations of psychiatric, psychological, social work or parole board interviews. Prison staff also can observe the manner in which the inmates express their character with each other, how they respond to letters and visits from their family, how they work, and how they react to various events in the prison community. This is in addition to the prospects for prison staff assessment of inmate employment capacities, already discussed.

A major problem for the parole board is how to benefit from this diverse staff knowledge. If complete acceptance were given to staff impressions of inmate attitudes, several risks would be involved. In the first place, the inmate adjustment to the prison situation, and his verbal expressions there, may not be indicative of his actual interest or ability to behave in any particular fashion outside of prison. The pressures and demands of prison life are much different from those of the outside community. Secondly, the ability of the staff to assess inmate attitudes from their expression in an institution varies tremendously. Indeed, research has shown that even prison employees who are professionally trained in the behavioural sciences, such as psychologists and psychiatrists, frequently are highly inaccurate in predicting the post-release conduct of prisoners. A final objection to automatic acceptance of staff assessments of inmates as a basis for parole decisions, is the fact that the personal involvement of staff with inmates may interfere with their objectivity in these assessments. Staff frequently develop a fondness for and a sense of obligation to aid those inmates who are affable and who are dependable workers. Conversely, they sometimes may be antagonised by other inmates who are withdrawn or who have unpleasant mannerisms. Yet these forms of behaviour in the institution may not be indicative of the inmate's prospects for achieving a non-criminal life on the outside.

Some parole boards deliberately refuse to accept definite prognoses or assessments on inmates from prison staff. Others insist on such reports, and attach considerable importance to them. The optimum policy appears to be to try to benefit from whatever valid knowledge may be gained from staff assessments, but to make a continuous effort to evaluate these assessments, and to do whatever may be possible to increase their validity.

These objectives suggest the following:

1. That independent reports should be secured from as many staff members as have extensive contact with the inmate, and that the extent of their contacts with the inmate should be indicated on their report.
2. That these reports should be structured as far as possible so as to indicate the specific kinds of observations on which the assessments are based. For example, they could describe the inmate's behaviour, and indicate the situation in which the behaviour was observed, rather than merely ascribe broad personal attributes to the inmate.
3. That these reports should also include comment on the associates the prisoner seems to have, and his relationship to these other prisoners.
4. That the report forms should be structured so as to obtain reports on both favourable and unfavourable attributes manifested by the inmate.
5. That staff should be informed that their reports will not necessarily determine parole board action, but will be pooled with a large variety of other information available in reaching action decisions.
6. That research should be undertaken to tabulate the prognostic significance of various types of statements in these staff assessments, by comparing the pre-release statements of staff with the post-release behaviour of the inmates assessed.

Relationships in the community

The ultimately crucial consideration in determining an offender's readiness for parole is evidence of his probable adjustment in the free community. As was shown, the ability of an inmate to get along well in prison may not be highly predictive of his behaviour in the free community, where he has many more alternatives of companionship, activity and responsibility to choose from, in many of which requirements for success are much different from those needed in prison. Some evidence of change in an offender's post-release prospects may come from reports on the inmate's relationships to outside persons while he is confined, as well as from his plans and arrangements for post-release life. Increasingly, evidence of outside adjustment potential is becoming available to parole boards through the temporary release of inmates prior to their outright parole.

Interest in the inmate's outside relationships, beyond that of considering this as an aid in judging the risks of parole, often significantly affects parole decisions. This additional interest is the compassionate concern which parole board members frequently have for the welfare of an inmate's family. In the National Parole Institute poll, 33.8% of the parole board members responding stated that concern for the inmate's family and dependents was one of the five most important considerations in their decisions to grant parole. Their median estimate of the proportion of cases in the preceding year in which this concern strongly influenced their decision was 9.2%.

Inmate ties with outside friends and relatives

A man's view of what he himself is like often stems from the reactions he gets from other persons. From the standpoint of modern social psychology, one would expect that an individual's conception of himself as criminal or non-criminal would depend very much on the types of persons whom he feels accept and respect him. Accordingly, it is very appropriate for the parole board to inquire about the types of friends a prisoner is likely to have on the outside. Especially important is some knowledge of the prisoner's relationships with his kin in the community to which he will be released, and the character of these relatives.

During periods when a person is involved in crime successfully, he often neglects and alienates much of his family, both those of blood descent and those by marriage. And, in this period he often makes or strengthens friendships among persons who accept, or even share, his criminality. Subsequent to his arrest and imprisonment, however, these relationships may change. There are two well-known sayings which may be appropriate here, but each seems to apply to a different type of associate.

One common expression is 'absence makes the heart grow fonder'. This seems to apply particularly to blood relatives of the inmate, especially parents. Frequently imprisonment occurs at the culmination of a long series of conflicts with parents and other relatives over difficulties in school and at work, in addition to conflict over his delinquency and crime. However, even inadequate and dissipated or criminal parents (and sometimes other kin), with impressive frequency, maintain a kernel of affection and sympathy which grows when separation dims the memory of old conflict. New hopes for the family's prodigal son often develop. The frequency of letters which prisoners receive from often not very educated relatives is noteworthy. Of course, such communication is inspired by the fact that imprisonment often is the first occasion when the offender shows time and interest in writing letters to them. Questionnaires addressed to prisoners asking them from whom they expect help on release have shown that the expectation of help from relatives distinctively increases the longer a man is confined in prison. It has also been shown repeatedly that the frequency of a prisoner's correspondence and visits from relatives is indicative of his probable post-release success.[14]

Another familiar saying is 'Out of sight, out of mind'. This seems to describe an inmate's relationship with his pre-prison friends, and frequently with his spouse. Prisons usually restrict letters and visits to an inmate from his friends, requiring some certification of the character of the friend, usually from one of the inmate's close relatives or other sources. Nevertheless, those friends – of either sex – permitted correspondence and visits with an inmate tend to communicate less frequently as time elapses. There also is a high rate of attrition in visits and correspondence from fiancées or wives to male prisoners (as well as from the corresponding relationship to female prisoners).

Many cases can be cited in which a youth was persistently involved in delinquent activities with friends of his own age from early adolescence until his late teens or early twenties, was frequently but briefly confined in detention homes, training schools or jails, and when released resumed his old relationships. Meanwhile his relatives became increasingly alienated from him. There are notable instances among such youth where a prison or reformatory confinement of several years at this advanced stage of a criminal career involved a change after a year or two, in which the inmate gradually reached a condition where the only friends he had left were his relatives. This is especially likely to occur as a change develops in his relationships in the prison, of diminishing involvement with the trust for fellow inmates, and increasing attachments to some of the staff with whom he has long and co-operative relationships.

Where a resocialisation and rehabilitation occurs in such cases during the course of imprisonment, the major factor appears to be the change in the other persons whom the inmate selects as his points of reference for looking at himself. This is to say, he comes to see himself from the standpoints of conventional persons, and defines himself as acceptable to them, in contrast with his prior practice of seeing himself only from the standpoints of his delinquent peers.

In those situations where a marriage relationship is maintained in spite of the strain of imprisonment over an extended period, the support of the spouse on release can be a major rehabilitative factor. Statistical studies in many jurisdictions have consistently found that the prospects of success for married parolees are much more favourable than those for single parolees. One study of the families of married prisoners has shown that while incarceration generally is a strain on marital ties, at least a third of the marriages of prisoners do not deteriorate during the husband's confinement, and in about one-tenth of the cases the ties between the husband and his wife improve when he is imprisoned.[15]

Most parole boards have some provision for hearing friends or relatives of inmates who are anxious to speak to the board, but parole boards generally prefer that communications from these persons be solely in writing because of the time involved in holding hearings for them. The contact with families may give the board a vivid personal impression that can arouse their sympathy with the inmate's dependents, or inspire disrespect and distrust for his family. While this may be a valuable revelation, it is important to try to validate impressions from hearings with as much objective knowledge on the character of the person heard and his relationship with the inmates as can be procured. It probably is easier to assess the inmate's probable post-release support or hindrance from relatives or friends from the record of their long-run relationship to him, from their loyalty to him during confinement, and from a pre-parole investigation of the inmate's prospective home, more adequately than from a brief contact at board hearings or from their correspondence with the board.

It may frequently be important for a parole board to be well informed and free of prejudice with respect to cultural aspects of the inmate's friendship or family relationships. It is found in a study in the state of Illinois, for example, that statistically speaking, relatives of Italian prisoners are especially loyal to the prisoners, while the relatives of Polish prisoners are more rejecting. Similarly parole board members should be aware of the high rate of illegitimacy and the relative lack of stigma such family ties connote in negro slum communities, as compared with communities where these patterns are almost unknown. If an inmate is strongly supported in pursuing a legitimate and self-sufficient life, this loyalty of another person may be a tremendous rehabilitative influence regardless of the legal nature of their relationship.

Pre-parole plans and arrangements

Over 90% of prisoners plan to return to the community where they resided before imprisonment and half expect to live in the homes of relatives at release. Although many returned parole violators blame their failure on their return to old locales, and some prisoners are anxious to be authorised release to what is for them a new community, statistically those who live with their relatives and those who return to their own community have higher success rates than other releases. The highest rates of failure on parole, in relationship to residence on release, is among those who live alone at release. Nevertheless, those who have discord with the persons with whom they reside have appreciably higher rates of failure on parole than those who adjust amicably with the persons with whom they live on release.

A significant proportion of released prisoners are completely dependent upon relatives for free or cheap room and board at release. This reflects the limited financial resources available to them when they leave the prison, the very many needs and desires for expenditures they have after a period of confinement, and the gap between the date of their release and that of their first pay cheque. Evidence that 'absence makes the heart grow fonder' was cited earlier with respect to relatives. It is also noteworthy that the proportion of inmates who say they expect harm from certain relatives or from other persons in their community, or who say they would refuse to accept help from certain people, declines during the period of confinement, especially as release approaches.[16]

Where an inmate is released to a home in which he previously had considerable discord with the other residents, and where he will again be living with them, it is probable that this discord will recur. Although all parties involved may expect a fresh and happy start on release, there is a tendency for early patterns in family relationships to repeat themselves. Much of this reflects the difficulties of youth in achieving a sense of independence and self-sufficiency. Often their recourse to criminal or disorderly associates reflects this striving for a conception of themselves as independent; with delinquents and criminals they feel more accepted as adults and more competent than they feel with conventional adults. Where there is a choice of relatives from whom the inmate can procure shelter and companionship during his first post-release months, it may be important to suggest that he select those with whom there is least prospect of interpersonal conflict for him. A sign of maturation in a youth, however, is the ability to tolerate discord, without reacting in self-destructive hostility. It is difficult to assess such maturation in the prison situation because the inmate and his relatives tend to idealise the future, regardless of what difficulties they have had in the past.

Pre-release job arrangement and trial release

Apart from the matter of post-release housing plans there is the problem of post-release employment arrangements. Many parole boards require that a job as well as a home be arranged for the parolee before he can be released on parole. In most cases a pre-release investigation of the prospective home and job is made by the parole supervision service. In the National Parole Institute survey of the opinions of parole board members, 53% agreed (24% 'very strongly agreed') with the statement: 'A prison inmate should not be paroled until assurance is provided that a suitable job is awaiting him upon release.' Twenty-eight per cent disagreed with this (18% disagreed 'very strongly'). The remainder had no opinion on this.

A number of inmates authorised parole are held beyond their release date when a satisfactory home and job cannot be procured for them. Nevertheless, studies in several jurisdictions suggest that pre-release arrangement of a parole job is not associated with markedly greater rates of success than release on parole without a prearranged job. This appears to reflect the high frequency of inadequate or totally spurious jobs arranged by prisoners in order to gain parole. There is a high rate of unemployment among newly released parolees regardless of whether or not they had a presumably bona fide job at release. Furthermore, the rate of return to crime is a direct function of the rate of post-release unemployment.[17]

All of these findings suggest that if pre-parole job arrangements are insisted upon, the utmost effort should be made to verify the adequacy of the job arrangements by means that go beyond the ordinary practice of simply having an employer agree in writing to hire the parolee. These agreements are often procured by the inmate's family as a basis for assuring his immediate release, and they are not legally binding on the employer. Where the employer is a long established firm with whom the inmate previously was successfully employed, the prospect of his being satisfactorily employed are optimum. However, these cases are a minority.

The New York Board of Parole initiated a 'Reasonable Assurance' release policy whereby any parolee could be released without a prearranged job if he had:

1. A stable home situation or other resources to assure his not becoming a public charge.
2. A marketable employment skill, and the capacity to solicit a job upon his arrival in the community through ordinary channels for securing employment there.
3. A community agency interested in helping him, if necessary. Independently of this, the Board also established Parole Employment Officers, at the major parole supervision offices, who are specialists in job procurement for released offenders.

Table 8.11 summarises the experience of the New York Board with various types of employment arrangements for those prisoners whom it released from June 1961 through December 1962. When there are many alternative methods of job procurement available to the inmate, as there are in New York, those who do get jobs on their own or through their family appear to be distinctly the best parole risks. Their success rate probably reflects not so much the job they get as their previous employment record, their reputation in the community and their family ties, all of which also enable them to get jobs without assistance. Those released without jobs but under the 'reasonable assurance' conditions described above did as well or better on parole than those procuring employment through parole staff. In addition, of course, this programme saves the state the cost of confinement and the impairment of inmate morale that normally results when there are many 'overdue' people in prison, that is, inmates confined beyond the date of their parole order because they lack approved job arrangements.[18]

Table 8.11

Parole violation rates by employment arrangements at release

Employment arrangement at release	Number of cases	Violation rate
Approved job developed exclusively by the inmate of his family	3,627	35·4
Approved job developed with aid of institution parole officer	55	43·6
Approved job developed by parole officer in the field	193	45·6
Approved job developed by parole employment officer in the field	1,727	47·8
Approved job developed by other means	49	32·7
'Reasonable assurance' release	1,192	43·6
Salvation Army or similar agency	42	42·9
School	13	23·1
Residence for female without gainful employment	21	52·4
All other, including parole to warrant	486	26·3
	7,405	39·4

Source: John M. Stanton, 'Is it safe to parole inmates without jobs?,' *Crime and Delinquency*, vol. 12, no. 2 (April 1966), p. 149.

An alternative solution to the employment arrangement problem is to provide pre-release furloughs for inmates, to enable them to seek jobs on their own. Those states which have tried this for many years with thousands of prisoners, for example

Michigan and Mississippi, have an almost 100% rate of return to the prison at the end of the furlough.[19] Also facilitating post-release employment are the Work Release programmes pioneered by North Carolina and growing in many jurisdiction states. These permit prisoners to depart daily to employment outside the prison, during as much as the last 5/6th of their prison term. Where work release is not to a job in the inmate's home community, job search assistance is more adequately provided by having the last few months of confinement served in a pre-release guidance centre, in the city to which the inmate will be released. These rapidly developing half-way institutions permit the prisoners to seek jobs, to start work on them, and to be counselled on their difficulties in job search or at work, before their parole begins. Since release is imminent in any case, society is much better protected when release is through these mechanisms to enhance prospects for subsequent self-sufficiency than when the inmate's release is abrupt. Trial releases by work, by furloughs, and especially by a pre-release guidance centre, provide a test of the readiness of the inmate to maintain himself in economic self-sufficiency in a legitimate manner. These programmes were the major new development of corrections in the 1960s in the United States.

It has been the experience of these centres that released prisoners, especially youths, have difficulty in holding jobs at first. This reflects both their lack of prior work experience in the free community, and the deficiency of prison work experience in comparison with work outside of prison. Sometimes it may reflect parolee personality problems, and even the personality problems of some parents, siblings or spouses. These relatives sometimes feel superior or have other personality needs met by the parolee's failure or by his dependence on them, and they may play unwitting psychological 'games' to encourage the parolee's failure. Added to all these problems of course, there often are clearly criminal orientations of some of the releases.

Methods of assessment of risk on parole

A parole board member can only judge a prisoner's prospects of further criminality by gathering whatever information and impressions he can, and interpreting their implications for further crime. He may use what he can learn about the individual before him to classify this person into some kind of type, so he can apply his knowledge or speculations to decide how likely it is that persons of that type would commit further crime if paroled under the expected circumstances. For example, the parole board member may know that a majority of the young auto thieves and most alcoholic forgers that have been paroled in the past have repeated their offences on parole. However, he usually finds that prisoners fit several categories in his typologies, or have unique features hard to classify. For instance, he may have a theory that persons who verbalise insight, and are favourably recommended by institution officials, generally are reformed, so he ponders how to apply this theory to an alcoholic forger. He may also have dozens of other facts and speculations as to specific factors as signs of probable future behaviour on parole. How does he integrate all these considerations?

One method of reaching a judgement as to a prisoner's probable future behaviour on parole is for the parole board member to follow his intuition. After he has gathered some information and impressions on the individual on whom he must make a decision, he just 'acts on his hunch'. He may not be certain why he decides as he does, although often a few features stand out for him in each case. This might be called the *Intuitive conclusion* method.

A second approach that many board members use is the *Systematic rating* method, in which they jot down favourable and unfavourable considerations on some kind of standardised form. These may be quite detailed forms, with plus and minus weights assigned to each entry, or they may be a broad outline with only a few headings. The latter was impressively used by a lecturer at a National Parole Institute, the psychiatrist Herbert Modlin of the Menninger Foundation. Dr Modlin talked of the desirability of summarising information into four main categories: (1) the prisoner's assets, (2) his liabilities, and also (3) the assets, and (4) the liabilities in the environment to which the prisoner is likely to be released.

As an exercise in the use of this rating sheet technique, the participants in the institute were divided into four groups, to consider one of the hypothetical cases employed in exercises at all of the institutes. In this exercise, one group of parole board members was asked to try to reach concensus and report only on the prisoner's personal liabilities, one only on his assets, and one only on the liabilities of the environment to which the prisoner would return, and the fourth only on the assets in this environment. The results were both informative and amusing. Each group saw only what it was looking for. The personal asset seekers noted that inmate's previous offences were not professional crimes, and that his work and behaviour in prison had improved markedly. The personal liability group focused on the psychologist's evaluation in the initial classification report, in which the inmate was called 'a typical case of early psychopathic personality'. The group seeking liabilities in the community noted that the inmate would be returning to the area in which his previous difficulty occurred, and that he would be living with his mother, whose over-indulgence and over-protection were said to be the cause of his character defects. The community assets group saw this quite differently. The inmate would be returning to a community in which he had employment and friends, and he would have a mother to comfort and assist him there.

This exercise demonstrated how one can readily see what one is looking for in any case material. Therefore one can intuitively be favourably or unfavourably impressed by an early perception in a case, then see only those aspects which confirm this initial reaction, and overlook other aspects. Systematic rating sheets may improve our assessment of individuals by forcing us to give some attention to both the positive and the negative aspects of each case.

A third method of reaching conclusions as to the probable future behaviour of an inmate is what might be called the *Statistical prediction* method. This is the way in which large insurance companies generally determine the risk in writing auto insurance. They know from previous experience that their costs in insuring a driver are likely to depend very much on the driver's age, sex, previous accident record, prior driver training, and perhaps a few other things that can be easily determined. Although auto accident rates actually depend on many subjective personality and situational conditions, each customer is given an insurance rate based just on the combination of objective statistical attributes by which the insurance company classifies him. They find this cheaper and more dependable than relying on an interviewer's judgement of a driver's accident proneness. This is essentially what statistical methods of parole prediction attempt to do.

In parole prediction the records of the prisoners paroled in past years are tabulated statistically to determine the violation rate for each group into which these past parolees could have been classified at release. Thus, separate violation rates are determined for each age, offence, prior criminal record, and other statistical categories. There are several methods of combining this information to get an overall prediction. One of the simplest procedures is to assign a 'parole success score' to each past parolee by giving him one point for each item on which he is in a category which had less than average violation rates, and either none, or minus points, for items in which he is in a category with above average violation rates. For example, a prisoner might get one point for being above 40 years old, one point for having the offence of manslaughter, one point for being a first offender, and so forth. Violation rates then are determined for each score; thus parolees with 12 points may have had only a 10% violation rate, as compared with 40% for those with only five favourable points and 80% for those with no points.

Using a statistical prediction method prisoners currently being heard for parole are classified by tables developed from statistical analysis of past experience. Thus a prediction report can be prepared for the board which might say: Prisoner Smith falls in a category with nine favourable points. 1968-1969 parolees with nine favourable points had a 20% violation rate.'

What method of case assessment should the parole board member use? Can he use more than one method? If so, how can he integrate these methods? To answer these questions we should know something of the accuracy of these separate methods, and then consider how this accuracy might be increased.

The accuracy of case assessment methods

It is probable that almost every parole board member actually uses elements of all three of these methods in reaching his decisions. He employs an often unwritten statistical method when he says to himself, 'This is the kind of inmate we've had pretty good luck with lately,' or 'This is a recidivist alcoholic forger, and four out of five of these fellows violate paroles.' He may use a case rating form, but if not, he is likely to jot down some notes in trying to reach his decision in many cases, and this may approximate the systematic rating sheet method. Finally, he integrates, in an intuitive conclusion, all his information, opinion and feeling on each case. The first step in improving case assessment is to know the extent and manner in which these different methods are used, the second is to analyse and assess the relative contributions of each method, and the third is to consider how these contributions can be improved, including how the several methods can be combined most effectively. Each parole board member must perform the first step himself; our concerns here are the second and third steps.

Surprisingly often, parole board members rely on ideas about the statistics of past experience which have no relation to actual statistics. Thus, at one National Parole Institute session, a parole board chairman said, 'I presume that most people paroled for rape are likely to rape again.' Few states have bothered to tabulate statistics on this matter, but they easily could. What data we have been able to find on this question, from the state of Pennsylvania, suggests that instead of 'most' paroled rapists repeating this offence, only about one per cent do.[20]

In the National Parole Institute questionnaire, a list of prisoner characteristics was presented, with an inquiry on whether each factor was favourable or unfavourable. Responses are summarised in Part A of Table 8.12. Next to this, in Part B, is a summary of actual statistical findings on violation rates for parolees with these characteristics, compared with average violation rates for all parolees in the correctional systems reporting to the Uniform Parole Reports.

On the whole, Table 8.12 demonstrates that there is a marked consistency between actual statistics and the predominant judgement of parole board members. The only appreciable discrepancies between judgement and fact were on age, narcotic addiction, and the crimes of homicide, rape, and armed robbery. Almost a third of the parole board members thought that a low age was associated with success on parole, although statistics from many jurisdictions consistently show the opposite. Also, violation rates for narcotic offenders have more often been found

Table 8.12

Opinions of 139 US parole board members and actual findings on success rates of parolees with selected characteristics

Prisoner characteristics	A. Per cent of Board members considering this item: Unfavourable	Neutral or indefinite	Favourable	B. Actual success rates, (or range, if findings are inconsistent in different states).
1. History of frequent intoxication	88.6	11.4	–	Low
2. Age 20 or less when up for parole	35.4	35.5	29.1	Low
3. Age 25 or more when up for parole	6.3	31.7	62.0	Average to high
4. Long delinquency record	81.0	17.7	1.3	Low
5. Parents divorced	41.8	56.9	1.3	Slightly low
6. Divorced from spouse	41.8	49.5	8.7	Slightly low
7. Left parental home at an early age	58.2	36.7	5.1	Low
8. Active interest by family	1.3	6.3	92.4	High
9. Narcotic violations	81.0	17.7	1.3	Average
10. Good prior work record	–	2.5	97.5	High
11. Inadequate prospective parole job	51.9	48.1	–	Low
12. Commitment for homicide	10.1	21.5	68.4	High
13. Commitment for forcible rape	55.7	29.1	15.2	High
14. Commitment for burglary	50.6	34.2	15.2	Low
15. Commitment for forgery	73.4	19.0	17.4	Low
16. Commitment for armed robbery	58.2	31.7	10.1	Average

Source: National Parole Institutes, 1965.

to be about average than above the average of an adult parole system. Armed robbery parolees have about average parole outcome rates, and both homicide and rape are associated with a high rate of success on parole.

In short, the findings were that although most parole board members are fairly well informed regarding available statistics on broad factors in parole outcome, an appreciable minority lacks this knowledge. However, they all make their predictive judgements in the course of deciding on individual cases, not on statistical categories. How accurate are their intuitive conclusions on individual cases? We can only know this when officials are willing to record definite predictions for each case which can be compared later with the actual post-release behaviour of the men on whom they made predictions. This has been carried out on only a few occasions. The results are interesting enough to suggest that it should be done more often.

In 1961 Ellis G. Savides, Associate Superintendent of Classification and Treatment at the California Department of Correction Medical Facility at Vacaville, reported his effort to check on case assessments. He interviewed 283 men when they were about to be released on parole, and studied their files, then rated them from zero to ten according to his judgement as to the probability of their success on parole. The results are summarised in Table 8.13.

He defined a 'favourable adjustment' on parole as one in which, within two years after release, the parolee was not sentenced to a new term of ninety days or more, was not returned to prison as a parole violator, and was not wanted as a violator at large.

Obviously, perfect prediction ability would permit him to divide men at release into two groups, in which all of one group would be successful and all of the other would be unsuccessful. Such perfection is not attainable for many reasons: the limits of our knowledge on the facts in each case, the need for further research on the relationship of known facts to parole outcome, and the infinite variability of humanity. However, the ideal of perfectly differentiating prospective parolees into a completely successful group and a completely unsuccessful group provides a standard; the available methods of case assessment can be evaluated by the extent to which they approach this standard.

Table 8.13 shows that, in an institution where only about half the parolees were able to make a successful post-release adjustment (as defined above), Savides was able to distinguish two low scores groups, comprising 19% of the releases, of whom only about a third later made a favourable adjustment. He also distinguished three high score groups, comprising 26% of the releases, of whom about two-thirds made a favourable adjustment. For the remaining 55% of the releases, whom he rated in the intermediate score groups, he could not predict very well.

Table 8.13

Savides' judgment of potential success, compared to actual adjustment of Vacaville parolees

Savides' success score	Cases assigned each score No.	%	% of cases in each score group actually adjusting favourably on parole
0	34	12	35
1	21	7	29
2	30	11	53
3	17	6	53
4	11	4	45
5	59	21	53
6	12	4	58
7	26	9	50
8	31	11	68
9	26	9	65
10	16	6	69
Totals	283	100%	52%

Source: Ellis G. Savides, 'A parole success prediction study', California Department of Corrections Research Newsletter, vol. 3, no. 3-4, (Sept.-Dec. 1961), pp. 4-10.

For the same 283 releasees, a predictive rating was made from the report of the 'clinical Council' of the Vacaville Institution. This council consisted of psychiatrists and psychologists. On the basis of these reports, Savides rated these inmates, before release, as either 'unfavourable', 'neutral', or 'favourable' with respect to probable parole adjustment. The council, as scored by Savides, rated only 21, or 7% of these 283 releases 'unfavourable', but nine of these 21, or 43%, actually had a favourable post-release adjustment, (using the criterion described above, that they were neither confined over ninety days, nor returned to prison, nor wanted for parole violation in their first two years on parole). On the other hand, the council gave a 'favourable' rating to 131, or 46% of the 283, and 65% of these actually achieved a favourable adjustment. Only 41% of the remaining cases rated 'neutral' had a favourable outcome. It is clear that Savides, using his own ratings, was more effective than the Council in distinguishing a clearly unfavourable group of releases, but by rating the Council's report he was able to identify a larger 'success' group, with about the same accuracy, (that is, about two-thirds actually adjusted favourably).[21]

These 283 releases are especially interesting because we also have a statistical prediction for them, based on tables derived from a prior follow-up study of the records of a representative sample of California adult male prison releases in 1956. This prior study derived scoring procedures by a complex statistical process known as ' multiple correlation'.

In this prior study, a large number of ways of classifying inmates by precommitment information were related statistically to parole outcome, and to each other. From these relationships it was calculated that the best prediction could be made by using only seven of these items. The seven items were combined into what was called a 'Base Expectancy Score' for each release, by giving him 21 points *plus*:

16 points if he had, in his arrest history, 5 or more years without arrest, or if he was a first offender.
13 points if he had no known history of opiate drug use.
8 points if his family members had no criminal record.
13 points if his offence was not forgery, 'bad cheques', or burglary.
And the number of points equal to six-tenths of his age.

Then, if appropriate, some points were *subtracted*:
3 points for each alias shown on his arrest record.
5 points for each previous incarceration.

Table 8.14 summarises the prediction by the Base Expectancy Table for those 283 Vacaville releases. It will be seen that no more than a third achieved a favourable adjustment among those with scores of less than 50, which comprise almost 40% of the 283 cases. Thus the Base Expectancy Table was more accurate than either Savides or the Clinical Council in identifying a group of prisoners with poor prospects for success on parole.

The Base Expectancy Tables also distinguished a group with scores of 70 or higher, comprising 28% of the total sample, of whom more than three-fourths actually made a favourable adjustment. Thus, the Base Expectancy Table did not distinguish as large a favourable outcome group as the Clinical Council did, but the cases in its favourable categories were more distinctly successful than those identified by the other assessment methods.[22]

Table 8.14

Base expectancy table prediction of potential success compared to actual adjustment of Vacaville parolees

Base expectancy score	Cases assigned each score No.	%	% of cases in each score group actually adjusting favourably on parole
0 to 9	3	1	33
10 to 19	5	2	0
20 to 29	12	4	17
30 to 39	38	13	32
40 to 49	54	19	33
50 to 59	50	18	44
60 to 69	41	14	58
70 to 79	26	9	77
80 to 89	36	13	89
90 or higher	18	6	94
Total	283	100%	52%

Source: Don M. Gottfredson, 'Comparing and combining subjective and objective parole predictions', California Department of Corrections Research Newsletter, vol. 3, no. 3-4 (Sept.-Dec., 1961), pp. 11-17.

An overall comparison of the several methods of case assessment applied to the Vacaville cases make it quite clear that in this particular trial, the statistical prediction method proved much superior to either source of intuitive conclusions, for distinguishing a large unfavourable group. The Clinical Council identified a larger group with clearly above the averarge success rates for Vacaville parolees, although the smaller favourable group identified by the prediction table was more markedly successful than the favourable groups distinguished by other methods.

Other comparisons of case study with statistical prediction procedures have had similar findings. Tests of alternative methods have been made with many types of prisons. In the ability to classify a large proportion of parole applicants into favourable categories which experience demonstrates have markedly above average success rates, and into unfavourable categories which prove to have markedly below average success rates, statistical prediction methods have been shown to be clearly more accurate than prognoses by psychiatrists, psychologists, sociologists, prison wardens or prison unit officers.[23]

However, no method of case assessment has come close to the idea of dividing all prisoners eligible for parole into one group which includes only failures, and another group which includes only successes. Furthermore, the task of parole boards in case assessment is more complicated than this. That is why all methods of case assessment are likely to be useful; each method has unique functions, and each can also be used to improve the other methods.

The complexities of case assessment objectives

Despite the superior accuracy of statistical prediction tables, such tables cannot solve the parole board's case assessment problems. There are many reasons for this.

One obvious limitation of such tables, at this writing, is that they have been kept fairly current and extensive only in a few jurisdictions. And even these tables could be considerably improved in the number of cases covered and information utilised. The situation varies across the nation. Many states have made no effort to develop such tables. Others have made small and sporadic tabulations.

As indicated, parole board members take many considerations into account in reaching their decisions. Furthermore, there are numerous aspects to what we found to be their primary concern, for example, whether the prisoner will commit a serious crime if paroled. Parole board members often are preoccupied not so much with the prospect of another crime being committed as with the kind of crime that may occur. Most boards will accept appreciable risk that some of their parolees will commit petty thefts or forgeries; they may assume that these risks would be even greater if the men were released by discharge, without the assistance and control which parole may provide. However, no board wishes to take marked risks that their parolees will commit violent offences, or enormous property crimes. No tables thus far developed have focused on these problems of determining the probability of specific kinds of parole outcome, rather than predicting some broadly defined parole success or failure.

In addition, parole boards are concerned not just with the probable post-release behaviour of a prisoner, but with the prospects that this behaviour will be better or worse if parole occurs at a different time. This is especially important in those jurisdictions where low minimum and high maximum sentences result in few releases from prison occurring by procedures other than parole. As most correctional systems increase the proportion of releases that occur with parole supervision, the prediction problem will more often be 'What is the optimum time for this prisoner's parole?' rather than 'Should the prisoner be paroled?'

A few prediction tabulations have been made to illuminate this complex question of the optimum parole date. In general, the research suggests that initially good risks become worse if long confined, but that advanced offenders become somewhat better risks after several years in prison.[24] But tabulations of this sort still are grossly inadequate for guiding case assessment. The most rigorous evaluation of the effects of different durations of confinement on parole outcome, for particular types of offenders, requires controlled experiments. In such research inmates classified in advance as of a given type would be randomly divided into groups that are released after different durations of confinement, without being aware of this random selection process. We have not evolved to this degree of experimentation in corrections, so we must deduce the effects of time confined by comparing the post-prison records of what we infer are similar offenders confined for different periods, or by theorising on the effects of imprisonment from our observations of prison life. This analysis of experience of interpretation of observation is done impressionistically in most cases, although it can be performed more systematically with rigorous record-keeping and analysis.

To many people, the overriding complexity in case assessment is the uniqueness of each individual. No two offenders are fully alike and no two situations to which they may be released are completely identical. Regardless of what the tables say, a parole board member sometimes believes that his information on a particular case is more significant for predictive purposes than the statistical conclusions about the category of offender in which the man is classified. Furthermore, other considerations that influence case decisions, like compassion for relatives, anticipated reaction in the community, and the other concerns summarised in Table 8.1 may have unique qualities in different cases. Prediction tables thus may seem to be incompatible with individualised treatment of each offender.

Actually, two ideas are intertwined in this concept of individualised treatment. The first is that each individual has somewhat unique problems with which the prison and parole staff may be able to help him. The casework approach to assistance emphasises investigating the subject's feelings as a person, and influencing him through unique personal relationships.

The second aspect of individualised treatment is diagnosis and prognosis. This is our concern here : how we assess an individual's probable behaviour under alternative decisions we might make regarding him. Here we also must try to understand each offender as a separate person, but we make our assessments by interpreting our view of him as an individual on the basis of our knowledge or feelings regarding the type of person we conceive him to be. In short, we relate him to types of other persons about whom we have acquired impressions and beliefs, from various sources. This means that analysis of each individual case is intricately connected with our analysis of groups of cases. That is why the improvement of individual case decisions depends on the systematic connection of each decision with experience in groups of past decisions.

Decision making and the violent offender

The problem of 'individual case' and 'statistical' decision making is often most clearly evidenced when parole boards are forced with parole decisions about violent offenders. Simply stated, there are two ways of making decisions as to how a given parolee is apt to behave in relation to some future event. These are : (*a*) knowing a great deal about the particular individual's behaviour in situations the individual sees as similar to the one we are predicting for; or, (*b*) knowing enough about the individual to be able to place him accurately in a group or class of individuals, a class whose behaviour in analogous situations we can specify fairly precisely.

For practical purposes, the second technique is all that is available for most decision making and may work extremely well, providing one has (*a*) defined the characteristics of the class or group so that the members really tend to behave similarly in similar situations, and (*b*) correctly identified the individual as indeed belonging to that group.

Two problems that arise in using clinicians as aids in decision making are that they, generally, are more used to the first technique (which means that accurate information can be available for only a few individuals) and have done relatively little of the painstaking work with large numbers necessary to make use of the second technique. Moreover, even prolonged contact with a given *individual* does not always fit one to prognosticate very effectively about him. For example, most psychiatrists estimate a patient by criteria they are most familiar with, such as fitness for therapy, extent and nature of psychopathology and so on, and these may have little pertinance to such matters as ability to hold a job or to function in a prison environment and so on.

Moreover, most murderers and violent offenders are poor, and most of the remainder are at best lower-middle-class. On the other hand, a clinician is usually most familiar with middle or upper-class people. These, as a rule, tend to have symptoms that consist of unpleasant feelings (such as anxiety, guilt, or depression) or certain complex behaviours, usually of a non-violent sort, such as school failure or sexual difficulties, which serve to mask or substitute for these feelings. Because middle-class people have strong prejudices against violence and many kinds of activities that conceal, to a certain extent, the existence of such unpleasant feelings, their neurotic problems seem very different from those of lower-class people. Lower-class people tend to do something *directly* about an unpleasant feeling, and, moreover, usually have less choice in the matter, because the opportunity for substitutive activities are less common.

The point of this observation is this: A psychiatrist who saw one of his middle-class patients hit someone else would often conclude, usually correctly, that something was badly wrong with the patient. If he made the same diagnosis at a fist fight in the slums he might well be wrong himself. There is no substitute for personal knowledge of the range of 'normal' and 'pathologic' behaviour in different social classes and different milieux. Moreover, people who 'feel' symptoms and people who 'act out' symptoms respond differently to treatment and really require quite different forms of treatments.

There is, in other words, no substitute for a clinician who has an intimate and ongoing relationship with (*a*) the kinds of cases seen by a parole board, (*b*) the kinds of questions that board members must have answered and (*c*) who has opportunity to help in devising other care and parole techniques.

Psychiatric counsel for a parole board, in dealing with persons having a record of violence, is likely to be especially useful where the crime involved does not seem to have been the expression of a subculture of violence. Where the crime was an act in which the offender simply behaved in the manner customary in his group for the situations in which the crime occurred (for example, where the crime was the reaction expected in the offender's social world in response to an insult in front of others) the psychiatrist's assessment may not add significantly to a parole board's ability to correctly predict future conduct.

Skilled and competent clinicians can help a parole board to decide whether a crime of violence was expressive of a persistent emotional disturbance likely to be manifested in further violence and the emotional state of those persons at the time of parole consideration. Different clinicians are likely to disagree on many cases if they make their assessments independently and then no one knows how accurate each may be. In cases considered especially important, the Board may wish to see if several sources of judgement agree.

The parole board must assess the clinicians available to them and consider what their experience has been with them for particular types of cases. This assessment may include learning how different clinicians differ in general optimism or pessimism regarding prospective behaviour for given types of prisoners, learning how they differ in language and emphasis, and how sound each has been in his past advice.

Of course, it is important to realise that some error in forecasting a prisoner's behaviour on parole may involve mistakes in predicting the parolee's probable post-release situation, rather than errors in assessing the offender, although the situations the offender gets into may often largely be determined by him. Nevertheless, both of these judgements are intertwined, and in the long run the overall accuracy of prediction is most important. However, the basic problem is that clinicians are asked to prognosticate in an area where no one is highly accurate for most cases, and where we frequently encounter difficulties inherent in any effort to predict a rare event.

The data from Pennsylvania, presented earlier, indicate that violent offenders are less likely than any other type of criminal to repeat the same offence, should they fail on parole. Indeed, only one homicide parolee in 250 (*0.4%*) repeated the crime of homicide, one sex offender in about 35 (*2.9%*) violated parole by another sex offence, and one assault case in 28 (*3.6%*) was returned to prison for assault. The highest rates of sex offence recidivism occurred following the non-violent sex offences, such as indecent liberties with children; these are offences which, of course, may be more shocking to most people than violent offences, and which sometimes lead to violence when the offender becomes panicky about the child reporting the offence.

Thus, those crimes which most concern parole boards are actually the least likely to be repeated on parole. It is the seriousness of offences involving violence, rather than their frequency on parole, which is the parole board's problem. Board members should be aware of the special difficulties involved in predicting a rare event, if they are to comprehend realistically their prospects for preventing a recurrence of violent crimes.

Even if a board were given all the psychiatrists, sociologists, statisticians, and other experts it desired to make a thorough investigation and analysis of each case, it is doubtful if it could achieve 80% accuracy in identifying the less-than-five-per-cent of parolees who commit clearly violent offences after release. Eighty per cent accuracy is about the greatest precision that has been demonstrated by any man or any prediction system, applied to a cross-section of prisoners, for predicting parole violation in general, rather than the more difficult task of predicting violence on parole. Of course, a board might sharply reduce the number of violent offences committed on parole if it stopped paroling, but this would merely mean releasing prisoners to commit violence as dischargees without the services of parole in facilitating a non-criminal life and restricting activities leading to crime.

If a board were 80% accurate in identifying the most violent parolees, they would still make more than two erroneous predictions in ten as long as the violence they sought to predict occurred in less than twenty per cent of the cases. This is simply a matter of mathematics. For example, if violence were committed by five per cent of prison releases in every thousand releases, a parole board would have to identify 50 men who would commit violence among 950 who would not. With eighty per cent predictive accuracy, we could expect the board to predict violence for twenty per cent of the 950, or 190 cases, and for eighty per cent of the 50, or 40 cases. However, in this total of 230 designations as probably violent, one could not know in advance which actually would be the 40 who would be violent. They would make a total of 200 erroneous predictions, the 190 non-violent designated as violent and the 10 violent not designated as violent, in identifying correctly the 230 cases in a thousand which include 40 of the 50 violence cases. These errors are apart from others they might make in predicting more common types of parole infraction, such as non-violent theft, burglary or return to narcotics.

The foregoing theoretical analysis assumes 80% accuracy in predicting violent parole infractions, and that five per cent of the men released will commit such infractions. If accuracy is lower, or the frequency of the behaviour to be predicted is less than five per cent, there will be more errors made in order to deny parole to a given proportion of those who would commit the predicted behaviour. If we had 80 or even 90% accuracy in predicting an event occurring in only one per cent of the cases, such as the commission of a violent sex offence by a paroled sex offender, our ratio of errors to correct predictions would be much greater than 200 to 40.[25]

If a board knew its accuracy in predicting violence on parole, it might decide approximately what proportion of non-violent potential releases it would be willing to keep imprisoned in order to reduce the release of those most likely to be violent. Presumably most boards willingly tolerate five or even ten or more errors in long confinement of probably non-violent persons to achieve each increase of one in the probably violent persons thereby confined. Of course, where these men are to be released by discharge if not paroled, parole can be justified as increasing society's protection through both the assistance and the surveillance it may bring to the release. Actually, predictive accuracy can be known only by recording predictions made on all cases before release, and making long-term tabulations of the relevance of these predictions to post-release behaviour. This has only been done in a few scattered instances.[26] Even this is only a rough estimate, for we only know our accuracy on those actually released; we can never have knowledge of the accuracy of predictions made on prisoners who were not released at approximately the time when our prediction was considered applicable. Only the experimental release of some randomly selected prisoners among those for whom predictions are unfavourable would test these predictions more fully.

Awareness of the inherent difficulty in predicting rare parolee behaviour without making many errors may not be comforting to parole board members after a parolee commits a violent crime, but it can provide some defences against second guesses. If a critic asks why a person who committed violence on parole was released, one can, of course, point to the favourable considerations on which the decision to release was based. If the critic refers to unfavourable information or recommendations in the case history, one generally can point to a large number of successful releases who also had these unpromising features in part of their prior case history.

Improvement of case assessment in parole

The first step in improving case assessments is to know their points of accuracy and of error. This can only be done by parole board members recording their case assessments as predictions of future behaviour, and also, recording the reasons for them. When they subsequently determine the accuracy of these predictions, they can see what factors were associated with correct and what with incorrect judgement. This may reveal kinds of cases or situations in which they are most accurate, and also those in which they are least accurate. These are obvious elements in any learning from experience.

At present every parole board member does this, but he does it haphazardly. By the time he has been on the board long enough to know the consequences of past decisions, his current decisions may be affected by experience, but he is likely to appraise past judgements only on the basis of the outcome of those cases which subsequently come to his attention. Usually these are only the cases which make notorious violations of the conditions of their parole. Those who are successful are not heard of again by the parole boards in most states, although a few parole boards improve their appraisal of past decisions by reviewing each case before granting discharge from parole.

The significance of prediction tables is that they provide a broad guide for the parole board member on what experience has been in past releases of individuals of various types. If a parole board member decides that for a given case special considerations of impressions make him predict behaviour in contradiction of the statistical conclusion, he should record this. If a parole board member decides that the statistical advice does not answer the questions he wishes to consider in an individual case (for example, the type of violation which is likely to occur, if any), he should also record this. Subsequent analysis of these records will provide a basis for redesigning prediction tables in the future.

Whenever a parole board member makes a prediction in contradiction to the statistical odds, it becomes appropriate for him to find out whether this increases the accuracy of his assessment or not. If, in subsequent analysis, the parole board member is found to make fewer errors of forecasting parole outcome than the prediction table would make, the special consideration recorded by the parole board member may indicate what new factors should be tabulated to improve statistical prediction, if minimally, when the table is least valid. On the other hand, if a parole board member finds that in certain types of cases he has a strong hunch in contradiction to statistical experience, but his hunches turn out to be wrong, the knowledge of these errors should prove enlightening to him.

A major limitation in all efforts to improve the assessment of parole cases is the fact that we only know the consequences of decisions to release a criminal; we never can determine the accuracy or error in decisions to order an inmate confined longer.

In the latter cases, experience after release does not tell us if the further criminality is lower than it would have been if release had occurred earlier. This applies both to statistical and case study judgements; we only can learn from that experience we are able to get. For this reason, the willingness of some parole boards to risk early release of certain offenders as an experiment can greatly improve our knowledge: (1) if careful records are kept on the subsequent behaviour of the released prisoners; (2) if those released earlier are randomly selected (to assure their comparability to those kept longer); (3) if records are kept on the types of prisoners from which the early release group is randomly picked, so that one can describe the types of prisoner to whom the experimental conclusions apply.

Notes

1 WEST Parole in England: an introductory explanation

1 *Report of the Parole Board for 1969*, London, HMSO, para. 39.
2 *Parole: Your Questions Answered*, London, HMSO, 1971.
3 *The Adult Offender*, London, HMSO, 1965, Cmnd 2852.
4 *Hansard*, House of Commons, 7.3.67, Col. 734.
5 *Hansard*, House of Commons, 26.4.67, Col. 1666.

2 WEST Parole in England: some comments on the system at work

1 *Hansard*, House of Lords, 17.2.71, Col. 640.
2 C. H. Rolph, 'Two cheers for parole', *Prison Service Journal 9*, 13-17, London, 1970.
3 In the Criminal Justice Bill, Nov. 1971, clause 27 gives the Home Secretary discretion to release on the direct recommendation of a Local Review Committee, without reference to the Parole Board.

3 MARTIN The Local Review Committee

1 *Hansard*, House of Commons, 12.12.66, Col. 206.
2 *Hansard*, House of Commons, 7.3.1967, Cols. 728-9.
3 *Ibid.*
4 *Report of the Parole Board for 1969*, London, HMSO, 1970. H.C. 48, § 80.
5 *Ibid.* § 82.
6 *Statutory Instrument 1967 No. 1462 Sec. 3.*
7 *Report of the Parole Board for 1968*, London, HMSO, 1969.
8 *Ibid.* § 94.
9 *Ibid.* § 94.
10 *Ibid.* § 94.
11 *Ibid.* § 91.
12 *Report of the Parole Board for 1969*, London, HMSO, 1970.
13 *Ibid.* § 75.
14 *Ibid.* § 58.
15 Hermann Mannheim and Leslie T. Wilkins, *Prediction Methods in Relation to Borstal Training*, London, HMSO 1955, pp. 121 ff.
16 *Report of the Parole Board for 1969, op. cit.*, § 26.
17 *The Adult Offender*, London, HMSO, 1965, Cmnd 2852.
18 *Report of the Parole Board for 1969, op. cit.*, § 93.
19 *Ibid.* § 88.

20 *Ibid.* § 62.
21 *Report of the Parole Board for 1968, op. cit.*, § 90.
22 *Report of the Parole Board for 1969, op. cit.*, Appendix 3.
23 *Ibid.*
24 *Ibid.* § 38.
25 *Report of the Parole Board for 1968, op. cit.*, § 85.
26 *Report of the Parole Board for 1969, op. cit.*, § 120.
27 If we imagine a simple case, without extensive police reports or court transcripts, the dossier is unlikely to be less than 20 pages. If only eight sets were produced this would entail 160 pages, while if twelve sets were produced the number would be 240. A round figure of 200 per case is not an unreasonable estimate. As 1835 cases were referred to the Board in 1969, the number of photocopy pages produced would probably have exceeded 350,000.

5 SHEA Parole philosophy in England and America

1 *American Law Institute Proceedings*, 33 Annual Meeting, Philadelphia 1956, p. 210.
2 Except for minor offences (misdemeanours and petty misdemeanours, MPC, § 6.08).
3 The categories of experts are listed in Schedule 2 to the CJA 1967.
4 The MPC (§ 402.1) only requires the members to be of good character and to have some experience in fields related to correctional administration and criminology. One member, in addition, has to be a member of the bar. The appointment is on a full-time basis.
5 18 months for England (CJA 1967, s.60 [1]); an indefinite term of imprisonment in excess of 1 year for the MPC (§ 6.10 [1]).
6 A similar solution exists in England only for young prisoners and prisoners serving an extended sentence.
7 *American Law Institute Proceedings*, 33 Annual Meeting, p. 275.
8 *Hansard*, House of Lords, 12.6.67, Col. 746/47.
9 An amendment approved by the May 1956 meeting to allow counsel at the actual hearing has again been dropped in the Proposed Official Draft.
10 The Board remains free to arrange a personal interview with the candidate should it consider it necessary (CJA 1967, s.59 [4b]).
11 *Report for the Parole Board for 1968*, p. 33.
12 For England: Board of Education v. Rice ([1911] A.C. 179). For U.S.A.: Morgan v. United States, 304 U.S.1 (1937).
13 See also: *Report of the Parole Board for 1969*, para. 112-15.
14 For reasons to opt out see: *Report of the Parole Board for 1968*, p. 19/20.
15 *American Law Institute Proceedings*, 33 Annual Meeting, p. 248.
16 *Report of the Parole Board for 1969*, p. 19.
17 In view of the fact that good behaviour in prison is only one and not necessarily a decisive factor in determining the date of release, this argument seems rather weak.
18 *American Law Institute Proceedings*, 33 Annual Meeting, Mr Rubin, p. 229.
19 (*a*) He [the parolee] must report, immediately upon release, to the officer in charge of the probation and after-care office at the address

specified in the licence. (*b*) He must place himself under the supervision of whichever probation officer is nominated for this purpose from time to time. (*c*) He must keep in touch with his probation officer in accordance with that officer's instructions. (*d*) He must inform his probation officer at once if he changes or loses his job.

20 American Law Institute, *Model Penal Code*, Tentative Draft No. 5, p. 10.

21 Parliamentary Debates, House of Commons, Standing Committee A, Criminal Justice Bill, Fourteenth Sitting, Tuesday 7th March, 1967, Col. 775. The only attempt made by two MPs (Sir J. Hobson and Mr Deeds) to spell out such conditions was unfortunately abandoned because they were considered to be an administrative matter: 'There is nothing at all in the Bill about that [the conditions]. It is correct that they should be imposed administratively, and I do not intend to debate on these Amendments what those conditions should be, because it is correct that they should be an administrative decision' (*Ibid*., Col. 774).

22 The central sentence simply reads: 'The conditions may be of a general kind, requiring the offender to report regularly to the probation officer and to lead an honest and industrious life, or they may be more specific such as the requirement to reside at a named hostel or at an address approved by the probation officer, or a requirement to undergo medical treatment.' (*Report of the Parole Board for 1968*, p. 10).

23 American Law Institute, *Model Penal Code*, Tentative Draft No. 5, p. 104.

24 'A probation order may in addition require the offender to comply during the whole or any part of the probation period with such requirements the court . . . considers necessary for securing the good conduct of the offender or for preventing a repetition by him of the same offence or the commission of other offences.'

25 R. Berger, *Le Système de Probation Anglais et le Sursis Continental*, Geneva, 1953, p. 9.

26 See H. W. R. Wade, *Administrative Law* s.98-131, Oxford, 1967.

27 Unfortunately the Parliamentary Debates do not give us any clue as to the purpose of s.62 (7); we therefore depend on mere suppositions. According to CJA 1967, s.62 (10) a parolee shall not be released after a judicial recall before the expiration of one year or before the expiration of one-third of the remaining parole period, whichever is the later.

28 *Report of the Parole Board for 1969*, Appendix 1, Table IV and V.

6 HAWKINS Some consequences of a parole system for prison management

1 A full account of the methods and results of this research will be found in my doctoral dissertation: 'Parole selection: the American experience', Cambridge University, 1971.

2 *The Adult Offender*, London, HMSO, 1965, Cmnd. 2852, para. 5.

3 *Ibid*. para. 5.

4 *Ibid*. para. 5.

5 G. M. Sykes, *The Society of Captives*, Princeton, 1958, p. 18.

6 *Ibid*. p. 21.

7 R. A. Cloward, 'Social control in the prison', in Cloward *et al*.,

Theoretical Studies in Social Organization of the Prison, New York, 1960, p. 48.

8 *Ibid.* p. 24.

9 Hawkins, *op. cit.* chs. 1 and 2.

10 G. M. Sykes and S. L. Messinger, 'The inmate social system', in Cloward *op. cit.* p. 13.

11 In states like California and Washington in which very high maximum terms are fixed by law, the parole boards have virtually no alternative but to grant parole to almost all their prisoners. But in these jurisdictions the question of when to parole takes on correspondingly greater significance than whom to parole, and the high maximum sentences still present ample opportunity to offer inducements to good behaviour and co-operation.

12 In almost all American states individuals are appointed to parole boards by the state governor. The commonest periods of tenure are four or six years.

13 New York, *Correction Law* (McKinney's, 1968), s. 213.

14 American Law Institute, *Model Penal Code* (P.O.D. 1962), s.305.9 (1) (*c*).

15 United States, Board of Parole *Rules*, Washington, D.C., 1965, p. 14.

16 D. R. Cressey, 'Limitations on organization of treatment in the modern prison', in Cloward *op. cit.*, p. 100.

17 Hawkins, *op. cit.* pp. 174, 218, 219.

18 D. R. Cressey, 'Sources of resistance to the use of offenders and ex-offenders in the correctional process', in Joint Commission on Correctional Manpower and Training, *Offenders as a Correctional Manpower Resource*, Washington, D.C., 1968, p. 45.

19 D. Jackson, 'Parole board', *Life* vol. 69. no. 2. (1970), p. 60.

20 *Ibid.* p. 59 (original italics).

21 D. A. Ward, 'Prison rule enforcement and changing organizational goals', unpubl. Ph.D. dissertation, University of Illinois, 1960, pp. 28-9.

22 Jackson *op. cit.* p. 61.

23 *Ibid.* p. 61.

24 California Adult Authority, *Parole: Philosophy, Policies and Program*, Sacramento, 1961, p. 17.

25 Hawkins, *op. cit.* p. 224.

26 *Ibid.* p. 226.

27 *Ibid.* p. 224.

28 R. McCleery, 'Communication patterns as bases of systems of authority and power', in Cloward, *op. cit.*, p. 56.

29 Hawkins, *op. cit.*, p. 226.

30 *Ibid.* p. 227.

31 *Report of the Parole Board for 1969*, London, HMSO 1970, H.C. Paper 48, paras. 112, 113. See generally Chapter V of this Report.

32 *Adult Offender, op. cit.*, para. 8.

33 Hawkins, *op. cit.* p. 229.

34 P. T. Takagi, 'Evaluation systems and adaptations in a formal organization: a case study of parole agency', unpubl. Ph.D. dissertation, Stanford University, 1969, p. 81.

35 Cressey, in Cloward *op. cit.* p. 101.

36 Hawkins, *op. cit.* pp. 219-20.

7 WALLER Parole for the ex-prisoner: carrot, stick or illusion?

1 It is not suggested here that the Adult Authority in California decides whether or not to release on the basis of treatment considerations, but that the Department of Corrections (which carries out parole supervision) has been interested in treatment possibilities. A review of public pronouncements from proponents of parole contained in annual reports, or statements by chairmen of parole boards, emphasise the value of parole as a method of treatment. For a history of both parole and parole research, see K. O. Hawkins, 'Parole Selection: the American experience', unpublished Ph.D. dissertation, Cambridge University, 1971, chs. 1, 2, 6, 9 and 10.

2 See S. Adams, 'Some findings from correctional case-load research', *Fed. Probation*, vol, 31, no. 4 (1967) pp. 48-57. The conclusions arrived at in this article should be read with caution: cost benefit advantages are not the same as treatment effects.

3 D. Clemmer, *The Prison Community*, New York, 1940. Only comparatively recently have sociologists extended their interest to other 'total institutions', such as hospitals, schools, etc. See, for example, E. Goffman, *Asylums: Essays on the Social Situation of Mental Patients and Other Inmates*, New York, 1961.

4 G. M. Sykes, *The Society of Captives*, Princeton, 1958; T. P. and P. Morris, *Pentonville: the Sociology of an English Prison*, London, 1963; T. E. Mathieson, *Defences of the Weak: a Sociological Study of a Norwegian Correctional Institution*, London, 1965; see also R. A. Cloward *et al.*, *Theoretical Studies in Social Organization of the Prison*, New York, 1960, and D. R. Cressey (ed.), *The Prison: Studies in Institutional Organization and Change*, New York, 1961.

5 H. Polsky, *Cottage Six*, New York, 1962; D. Street *et al.*, *Organisation for Treatment, A Comparative Study of Institutions for Delinquents*, New York, 1966.

6 A. V. Huffman, 'Problems precipitated by homosexual approaches on youthful first offenders', *J. of Social Therapy*, vol. 17, p. 216-22 (1961); J. Herbert, *Fortune and Men's Eyes*, New York, 1968.

7 Deprivation of liberty, of course, is a punishment in itself. The significance of degradation in this discussion is first in whether it has any long-term effects, and, if so, in the proportion of prisoners affected by it. See also S. Wheeler, 'Socialization in correctional communities', *Am. Sociological Rev.*, vol. 26 no. 5 (1961), pp. 697-712.

8 D. Glaser and J. Stratton, 'Measuring inmate change in prison', in Cressey (ed.), *The Prison*, *op. cit.*, pp. 381-92.

9 J. Irwin and D. R. Cressey, 'Thieves, convicts and the inmate culture', *Social Problems*, vol. 10 no. 2 (1962), pp. 142-55.

10 P. T. Takagi, *Criminal Types in Parole Prediction – Attitude Change on Parole*, California Department of Corrections, Research Report no. 14, Sacramento, 1965; A. N. Himelson and P. T. Takagi, *Parole Panel Study. Report A: Theory and Method with Comparison of Experimental and Control Subjects*, California Department of Corrections, Research Report no. 7, Sacramento, 1963. See also Irwin and Cressey, *Social Problems, 10, op. cit.*, pp. 142-55, and J. Irwin, *The Felon*, Englewood Cliffs, 1970, *passim*.

11 D. Glaser, *The Effectiveness of a Prison and Parole System*, Indianapolis, 1964.

12 *Ibid.* p. 390.

13 *Ibid.* p. 391.

14 J. H. Skolnick, 'Towards a developmental theory of parole', *Am. Sociological Rev.*, vol. 25 no. 4 (1960), pp. 542-9. Skolnick points out that he does not pretend to solve completely the methodological problems which would be involved in carrying out relevant research. As such, Skolnick's is typical of theories not developed in close relationship to the data; he did, however, try to construct hypotheses which could be tested.

15 See, for instance, the expectations of occupational advance by the prisoners studied by Glaser, in *Effectiveness of a Prison and Parole System, op. cit.*, pp. 311-16. See also D. A. Strathy, 'The expectations of the parole supervision experience held by penitentiary inmates prior to their release on parole' (unpublished M.S.W. thesis, University of Toronto, 1961) for some of the problems and results produced by testing some of the hypotheses put forward by Skolnick.

16 R. M. Martinson, G. G. Kassebaum and D. A. Ward, 'A critique of research in parole', *Fed. Probation*, vol. 28, no. 3 (1964), pp. 34-8.

17 E. Studt, *Re-entry of the Offender into the Community*, Washington, D.C., 1967.

18 H. Garfinkel, 'Conditions of successful degradation ceremonies', *Am. J. Sociology*, vol. 61 March (1956), pp. 420-4; T. R. Sarbin, 'The dangerous individual: an outcome of social identity transformations', *Brit. J. Criminol.*, vol. 7 no. 3 (1967), pp. 285-95; Studt, *Re-entry of the Offender*. Studt is also applying these ideas to the parole system she is studying in connection with her own research.

19 J. Havel and E. Sulka, *Special Intensive Parole Unit: Phase Three*, California Department of Corrections, Research Report no. 3, Sacramento, 1962.

20 J. Havel, *Special Intensive Parole Unit: Phase Four – the Parole Outcome Study*, California Department of Corrections, Research Report no. 13, Sacramento, 1965.

21 See F. Zimring and G. Hawkins, 'Deterrence and marginal groups', *J. of Research in Crime and Delinquency*, vol. 5 no. 2 (1968), pp. 100-14. This is one of the few pieces of published research so far to have emerged from extensive studies of deterrence being carried out in the Center for Studies in Criminal Justice at the University of Chicago. See also H. D. Willock, 'Deterrents and incentives to crime amongst youths aged 15 to 21 years', unpublished report (1967) prepared for the Home Office by the Social Survey.

22 J. D. and M. Q. Grant, 'A group dynamics approach to the treatment of non-conformists in the navy', *The Annals of the American Academy of Political and Socal Science*, vol. 332 (1959), pp. 126-35.

23 The discussion in the section on the 'Decision to Revoke Parole' (below) emphasises factors other than the behaviour of the parolee which can influence the revocation decision.

24 While every conviction for felony may not provide a very satisfactory measure as there are many factors which contribute unreliability, such as plea-bargaining or the charge which the police decide to bring, these should apply equally to both parolees under intensive supervision and controls under standard supervision.

25 R. G. Hood and R. F. Sparks, *Key Issues in Criminology*, London and

New York, 1970, ch. 7: 'Interaction between type of treatment and type of offender'.

26 S. Adams, 'Interaction between individual interview therapy and treatment amenability in older Youth Authority wards' in *Enquiries Concerning Kinds of Treatments for Kinds of Delinquents*, California Board of Corrections, Monograph no. 2, Sacramento, 1961.

27 R. H. Hall *et al.*, *A Descriptive and Comparative Study of Recidivism in Pre-release Guidance Center Releases*, U.S. Bureau of Prisons, special projects on work release, Washington, D.C., 1966.

28 Glaser, *Effectiveness of a Prison and Parole System*, pp. 292-301.

29 See J. Robison *et al.*, 'A review and new findings: offender classification, sentencing, disposition, supervisor intensity, violation rate', Final report of *The San Francisco Project: A Study of Federal Probation and Parole*, Berkeley, 1969, particularly pp. 32-42.

30 California provides numerous examples of programmes mounted taking this type of effect into account through cost-benefit procedures.

31 Havel and Sulka, *S.I.P.U. Phase Three*, *op. cit.*, p. 7.

32 This assumes that one can apply rational models to the administration of criminal justice. This idyllic situation does not even exist in California, though the 'Work Unit' and 'Probation Subsidy' projects are near equivalents. In this connection see R. A. McGee, *The Organization of State Correctional Services in the Control and Treatment of Crime and Delinquency*, Sacramento, 1967.

33 The study is, perhaps, able to draw some conclusions about probation officer activity.

34 This table is taken from J. Lohman *et al.* 'The intensive supervision case-load', Research Report no. 11 of *The San Francisco Project*, Berkeley, 1967.

35 P. T. Takagi, 'The effect of parole agents' judgements on recidivism rates', *Psychiatry*, vol. 32 no. 2 (1969), pp. 192-9; P. T. Takagi and J. Robison, 'The parole violator: an organizational reject', *J. of Research in Crime and Delinquency*, vol. 6 no. 1 (1969), pp. 78-86; J. Robison and P. T. Takagi, *Case Decisions in a State Parole System*, Sacramento, State of California: Research Division, California Department of Corrections, 1968, Research Report No. 31.

36 See R. G. Hood, *Sentencing in Magistrates' Courts*, London, 1962; J. Hogarth, *Sentencing as a Human Process*, Toronto, 1971.

37 P. T. Takagi, *Psychiatry*, vol. 32, p. 198. P. T. Takagi and J. Robison, *J. of Research in Crime and Delinquency*, vol. 6, p. 85.

38 P. T. Takagi, 'Evaluation systems and adaptations in a formal organization: a case study of a parole agency', unpublished Ph.D. dissertation, Stanford University, 1967.

39 *Ibid.* ch. 5. The parole administrator also went round the offices emphasising the importance of keeping men on the street.

40 *Ibid.* pp. 163-4.

41 J. Robison, '2943 PC decision making study – a preliminary analysis', unpublished paper from [California Department of Corrections] Bay Area Research Unit. See also J. Robison *et al.* 'It's time to stop counting', California *Prison, Parole and Probation System Technical Supplement no. 2*, Sacramento, 1969.

42 Takagi, *Evaluation Systems*, *op. cit.*, p. 167. See also J. Robison, M. Fagerstrom, R. Kingsnorth, J. Blunck, M. Kevorkian, *Two Years on Continuous Parole: A Description of Subjects Considered for Discharge*

During Early Implementation of 2943 PC, (Working paper, March, 1967, of Bay Area Research Unit), p. 16, for an interesting example of the importance of *characterisation* by the parole supervisor as opposed to the *characteristics* of parolees in relation to the decision to discharge from parole.

43 D. A. Ward, 'Evaluation of correctional treatment: some implications of negative findings', in S. A. Yefsky (ed.), *Law Enforcement Science and Technology*, New York, 1967, pp. 201-14.

44 These problems result from evaluative research, where 'double blind' methods are not used. In the S.I.P.U. studies the parole supervisors knew they were being studied and knew on which parolees they needed to have an impact.

45 J. Havel, *Special Intensive Parole Unit: Phase Four 'The Parole Outcome Study'*, California Department of Corrections, Research Report No. 13, Sacramento, 1965. See also S.I.P.U. *'High Base Expectancy Study'*, Research Report No. 10.

46 Adams, *Fed. Probation*, *31*, pp. 48-56; R. G. Hood, 'Research on the effectiveness of punishments and treatments' in *Collected Studies in Criminological Research*, vol. 1, Strasbourg, 1967, pp. 73-104; R. F. Sparks, 'Research on probation, parole and measures of after-care', Strasbourg, 1968. The substance of the latter two reports is contained in Hood and Sparks, *Key Issues*, *op. cit.*, chs. 6 and 7.

47 For an interesting exception, see the unpublished progress reports of the work by J. Ciale *et al.* carried out at the Department of Criminology, University of Montreal, on comparisons between parolees and men released at expiration of sentence.

48 See, for instance, B. M. Johnson, *Parole Agent Job Analysis*, California Youth Authority, Research Report no. 19, Sacramento, 1961; J. F. MacGregor and M. E. Fowler, 'Work time demands on parole agents: a work sample study', unpublished rough draft, California Department of Corrections, 1965; A. P. Miles, *A Time-study of Wisconsin Probation and Parole Agents*, Winconsin Division of Corrections Research Report, Madison, 1964.

49 Robison, *California Prison, Parole and Probation System*, *op. cit.*, Technical Supplement no. 2, p. 81.

50 Polsky, *Cottage Six*, *op. cit.*, p. 166.

51 See, for example, N. R. Arluke, 'A summary of parole rules – thirteen years later', *Crime and Delinquency*, vol. 15 no. 2 (1969), pp. 267-74.

52 See, for instance, S. K. Hunt, 'The revocation decision: a study of probation and parole agents' discretion', unpublished M.S. dissertation, University of Wisconsin, 1964.

53 D. M. Gallart *et al.*, 'Enforced clinic treatment of paroled criminal alcoholics', *Q. J. of Studies on Alcohol*, vol. 29 (1968), pp. 77-83.

54 See, for instance, S. B. Guze *et al.*, 'Psychiatric illness and crime with particular reference to alcoholism: a study of 223 criminals', *J. of Nervous and Mental Disease*, vol. 134 no. 6 (1962), pp. 512-21.

8 O'LEARY The assessment of risk in parole decision making

1 For a description of the variety of considerations in a parole decision in three jurisdictions see Robert O. Dawson, *Sentencing: The Decision as to Type, Length and Conditions of Sentence*, Boston, 1969, pp. 261-98.

2 The questionnaire was compiled in 1965 by the National Parole Institutes an organization jointly sponsored by the U.S. Council of State Governments, the National Council on Crime and Delinquency, the Association of Parolling Authorities, and the U.S. Parole Board.

3 Training session for new parole board members in the fifty states of the U.S. have been conducted periodically by the National Parole Institutes since 1963.

4 Portions of the material concerning pre-incarceration characteristics was previously published by the authors in a monograph *Personal Characteristics and Parole Outcome*, Washington, D.C., U.S. Department of Health, Education and Welfare, 1966. The data from the Uniform Parole Reports, another programme of the National Parole Institutes was not available at that time, however, and was not included.

5 Thorsten Sellin, 'Recidivism and maturation', *National Probation and Parole Association Journal*, vol. 4, no. 3 (July 1958), pp. 241-50; Barbara Wooton, *Social Science and Social Pathology*, New York, 1959, Chapter 5; Daniel Glaser, *The Effectiveness of a Prison and Parole System*, Indianapolis, 1964, pp. 36-41. See also, California Director of Corrections and Adult Authority, *California Male Prisoners Released on Parole 1946-49*, p. 23 and p. 46 (Tables 7 and 31). These tables indicate felony and misdemeanour violations separately, for first paroles and for reparoles, by year of birth.

6 Wooton, *op. cit.*

7 George B. Vold, *Prediction Methods and Parole*, Hanover, N.H., 1931.

8 Sydney Axelrad, 'Negro and white male institutionalized delinquents', *American Journal of Sociology*, vol. 47, no. 6 (May, 1952), pp. 569-74; Henry Al Bullock, 'Significance of the racial factor in the length of prison sentences', *Journal of Criminal Law, Criminology, and Police Science*, vol. 52, no. 4 (Nov.-Dec., 1961), pp. 411-17.

9 See Daniel Glaser, 'A reformulation and testing of parole prediction factors', Ph.D. dissertation, University of Chicago, 1954.

10 See Keith A. Coombs, 'An analysis of the Academic Educational Program in Washington State Adult Correctional Institutions', State of Washington Department of Institutions (Olympia, Wash.) *Research Review*, no. xx (June 1965); *Wisconsin Base Expectancies for Adult Male Parolees*, Progress Report no. 6, Madison, Wisconsin, Department of Public Welfare, Bureau of Research, (November 25, 1964).

11 See Robert M. Harrison and Paul F. C. Mueller, *Clue-Hunting About Group Counselling and Parole Outcome*, Sacramento, California, Department of Corrections, Research Report no. 11, 1964.

12 Evelyn S. Guttman, *Effects of Short-Term Psychiatric Treatment on Boys in Two California Youth Authority Institutions*, Sacramento, California, Department of the Youth Authority Research Report no. 36, (December 1963).

13 Stuart Adams, 'Interaction between individual interview therapy and treatment amenability in older youth authority wards', in California Board of Corrections Monograph no. 2, *Inquiries Concerning Kinds of Treatments for Kinds of Delinquents*, Sacramento, 1961, pp. 27-44, republished in Norman Johnston, *et al.*, *The Sociology of Punishment and Correction*, New York, 1962, pp. 213-24.

14 Lloyd Ohlin, 'The stability and validity of parole experience tables', Ph.D. dissertation, University of Chicago, 1954.

15 Pauline Morris, *Prisoners and Their Families*, New York, 1965.

16 Glaser, *Effectiveness of a Prison and Parole System*, *op. cit.*, pp. 374-88.

17 *Ibid.*, pp. 321-30.

18 John M. Stanton, 'Is it safe to parole inmates without jobs?', *Crime and Delinquency*, vol. 12, no. 2 (April 1966), p. 149.

19 See Robert H. Scott, 'Passes and furloughs', *American Journal of Correction*, vol. 27, no. 1 (January-February 1965), p. 30.

20 William L. Jacks, 'Trends of sex offenders over fifteen years', Harrisburg, Pennsylvania Board of Parole, Feb. 7, 1963.

21 Ellis G. Savides, 'A parole success prediction study', California Department of Corrections *Research Newsletter*, vol. 3, no. 3-4 (Sept.-Dec. 1961), pp. 4-10.

22 Don M. Gottfredson, 'Comparing and combining subjective and objective parole predictions', California Department of Corrections Research Newsletter, vol. 3, no. 3-4 (Sept.-Dec., 1961), pp. 11-17. The base expectancy method used is reported in Don M. Gottfredson and Robert F. Beverly, 'Development and operational use of prediction methods in correctional work', *Proceedings of the Social Statistics Section of the American Statistical Association*, Washington, American Statistical Association, 1962.

23 For statistics from other comparisons see Hermann Mannheim and Leslie T. Wilkins, *Prediction Methods in Relation to Borstal Training*, London, HMSO, 1955, pp. 158-60, 170, and Appendix V; Harrison G. Gough, 'Clinical versus statistical prediction in psychology', ch. 9 in L. J. Postman (ed.), *Psychology in the Making*, New York, 1962.

24 Cf. Donald L. Garrity, 'The prison as a rehabilitation agency', and Chapter 9 in D. R. Cressey (ed.), *The Prison: Studies in Institutional Organization and Change*, New York, 1961.

25 The difficulty of predicting a rare event is known in statistical decision theory as the problem of antecedent probability, or the 'base rates' problem. For a detailed analysis see Paul E. Meehl and Albert Rosen, 'Antecedent probability and the efficiency of psychometric signs, patterns or cutting scores', *Psychological Bulletin*, vol. 52 no. 3, May 1955, pp. 194-216.

26 For example, see Don M. Gottfredson, 'Comparing and combining subjective and objective parole predictions', California Department of Corrections, Research Newsletter, Sept.-Dec., 1961, pp. 11-17.

Index

Adams, S., 129
The Adult Offender (White Paper), 18, 48, 74, 97, 112
After-care hostels, 49, 59, 62, 63, 179
After-care service, 25, 34, 36, 58-65, 179
Age of offenders, 12, 18, 140, 142, 144, 183, 184
Alcoholics Anonymous, 105, 165
Alcoholism, 62, 83, 105, 120, 131, 132, 134, 142, 145, 180, 183, 184
American Law Institute, 66, 67, 69, 73, 74, 85
American Parole Board, 70, 74, 76, 81
American Parole Board Membership, 71
Ashwell Prison Magazine, 20
Auto theft, 144, 145, 147, 180

Borstal, 36, 47, 49, 56

California Community Treatment Project, 123-4
Californian System, 117, 118, 122, 124, 155, 163, 164
Californian System Adult Authority, 117
California Work Unit, 124
Capital punishment, 30
Casework, 21, 28, 116, 122-6, 132 134, 189, 191
Case histories (individual), 103-6, 114, 115, 126, 165
Clemmer, D., 119
Cloward, R. A., 98
Community care, 59, 61, 62, 175, 176, 181
Conviction records, 141-3
Cressey, D. R., 104, 113, 119
Crime, prior involvement, 141-3, 155, 156, 157, 159
Criminal Justice Act, 1948, 84-5
Criminal Justice Act, 1961, 23
Criminal Justice Act, 1967, 11, 12, 14, 66, 67, 70, 72, 74, 75, 76, 81, 83, 86-9, 93, 94

Dangerous offenders, 23, 24, 50, 64, 65, 88, 103, 144, 146, 147, 183-5, 191-6
Davis, M., *The First Parolees*, 65
Delinquents, 122, 131, 141, 150, 173, 176, 184
Department of Natural Resources, 113
Devel Vocational Institution, 164
Drugs, 62, 118, 120, 131, 144, 146, 147, 183, 184, 195

Employment problems, 59, 120, 121, 131, 133, 134, 149, 162, 168, 176-9, 184
Extended sentence cases, 12, 24

Family ties, 42, 60, 63, 65, 83, 120, 121, 132, 134, 137, 151, 172-9, 184

Gambling, 62, 83, 131, 143
Garfinkel, H., 121
Glaser, D., 120
Grant, J. D. and M. Q., 122
Grendon Psychiatric Prison, 49, 50

Half-way houses, see After-care hostels
Hall, R. H., 123
Havel, J., 128, 129
Henderson Hospital, 62
High security prisons, 29, 119
Higher Criminal Courts, 86-8
Himelson, A. N., 119

Homelessness, 59-61, 121, 176
Home Office, 15-17, 23, 25, 28-31, 39, 41, 51, 83, 85, 94
Home Office:
  Memorandum *Life Sentence,* 91
  Parole Unit, 13-15, 27, 41, 46, 47, 56, 71, 75
  Prison Department of, 12
  Research Unit, 52, 54, 65
Home Secretary:
  12-19, 25, 29, 33, 41, 71, 72, 80-2
  Recall powers of, 86, 87, 88, 90, 92, 93
Homicide, 144, 146-8, 153, 183-5, 194
Hood, R. G., 123, 129
Hostels, 12, 49, 60, 82
Hunt, Lord, 14, 20, 23, 24

Illegal service crimes, 143
Imprisonment, duration of, 11, 12, 22-3, 72-3, 89, 98, 152-6
Intelligence tests, 149, 150
Interviewing, 13, 17, 28, 39-43, 50, 56, 75, 76, 94, 99, 105, 115
Iremonger, T. L., 33, 34, 35, 37, 38
Irwin, J., 119

Jacks, W. L., 146
Jenkins, R., 18, 19, 83
Johnson, L. B., 62
Jones, Sir E., 32

Kassebaum, 121

Leave of absence, 12
Legal rights (of parolees), 17, 70, 75-8, 93, 127
Life sentence offenders, 18, 30, 31, 50, 51, 72, 80, 81
Local Review Committees, 13-18, 20, 15, 17-29, 31-57, 71, 94
Local Review Committee: reports to, 39
Local Review Committee Rules 1967, 39-41, 83
Local Review Committee: training for members, 54
Long-term offenders, 22-4, 30, 31, 50, 72, 80, 97
Lord Chief Justice, 18, 26

Magistrates, 37, 39, 88, 127
Mannheim, H. and Wilkins, L. T., *Prediction Methods in Relation to Borstal Training*, 47
Martinson, R. M., 121
Messinger, S. L., 98
Ministry of Labour, 59
Ministry of Social Security, 58, 59
Model Penal Code, 66, 67, 69, 70, 72-86, 89, 91, 93, 94, 101
Modlin, Dr H., 180
Morris, P., 119
Morris, T. P., 119
McCleery, R., 109

Narcotics, see Drugs
National Conferences, 53, 54
National Parole Institutes, 135, 152, 172, 176, 180, 183
New York Board of Parole, 177
Nelles School, 164

Offence categories, 143-8, 180
Offenders, physical appearance of, 148
Out-working schemes, 49
Open prisons, 28, 52

Parole:
  aims of, 68, 69, 70, 79, 96, 97, 99, 101, 160
  as means of correction, 98, 99, 101, 102, 105, 106, 108-10, 121, 122, 129, 132, 160
  as reward, 107, 110
  conditions of, 13-20, 23, 25, 51, 72-5, 81-5, 135-98
  effect on prison community, 97, 102, 103, 107, 114, 137
  failure rate, 51, 64, 65, 116, 122, 123, 125-7, 142, 144, 156, 168, 175
  Form LB2, 36
  licences, 16-18, 25, 73, 79, 82, 83, 87, 88, 131, 132
  prediction ratings, 180-9, 195-8
  prediction studies, 118, 140-52
  risk to community, 100, 101, 124, 133, 134, 171, 172
  supervisor, 17, 22, 26, 34, 35, 120-2, 125, 127-37
Parole Board:
  Annual Reports, 19, 21, 22, 29,

30, 45, 49, 52, 55, 83, 84, 91, 111
Chairman, 14
contact with families of parolees, 174
membership, 14, 24, 27, 35, 37, 38, 71
membership training sessions, 139
panels, 15, 27, 38, 39, 43-8
recall powers of, 86-90, 92, 94, 117, 126, 128
Parolees:
class differences, 192-3
intensive supervision of, 124, 125, 128, 130, 131, 155
rehabilitation of, 58-65, 70, 84, 99, 104, 115, 116, 121, 124, 130, 131, 134, 175, 185, 186
sex of, 148-9
wives of, 60, 63, 133, 173, 174
Partial release, 12
'Peak' effect of imprisonment, 48-9, 97, 153
Pennsylvania Board of Parole, 146-7
Police reports, 45, 46, 48
Polsky, H., 119, 131
Predatory crimes, 143-6
Preston School of Industry, California, 164
Prison:
Board of Visitors, 13, 32, 39, 48
Case Officers, 44-5
chaplain, 165
discipline, 47, 48, 80, 98-9, 102-4, 108, 114, 156-60
education courses, 160-3, 165
governors, 13, 24, 32, 34, 38, 39, 44, 48, 137
hostels, 49
morale, 47, 48, 51, 107-11
population control, 97, 111-13
Welfare Officers, 35-9, 44, 45, 55, 57, 61
work programmes, 59, 105, 106, 110, 112, 113, 120, 161, 166-9
Prisoners:
abnormal, 23
communications with, 28, 35-8, 40-3, 45, 50, 55, 76, 100
conduct motivation, 101-7, 109, 110, 150, 161, 165, 167
co-operation, 104, 105, 107, 110
dependants of, 21, 63
group counselling, 105, 110, 118, 163-6
inmate role, 118-20
misconduct of, 102, 103, 106, 156-60
rehabilitation of, 98, 102, 105-7, 112, 160-9, 174
records, 13, 24, 41, 102, 111, 139, 157, 159, 167, 169, 171
Wives Groups, 63
Probation, 85, 116, 117, 130
Probation Officers, 11, 15, 21, 25, 26, 34-35, 39, 40, 46, 55, 58-62, 64, 65, 82, 84, 87
Proposed Official Draft, 81
Prostitution, 143
Psychiatric reports, 110, 164, 170, 189, 192-4
Public opinion, 133, 135, 146, 153
Punishment, aims of, 68, 98

Race, 150, 151, 175
Rape, 144, 146, 183, 185
Recalled offenders, 17, 18, 54, 65, 76, 80, 85-94, 117, 127, 128, 130, 147, 150, 154, 178, 183
Reconviction:
expectancy, 29, 129, 142-50, 153, 155, 157-98
influence of, 129-33, 136
risks, 51, 79, 118, 125, 126, 138, 139, 147, 183, 189, 190
References for prisoners, 42
Refusal to accept parole, 78, 86
Release date, 22
Religion, 20, 165, 166
Remission, 11-13, 98, 99, 101
Robison, J., 126, 128, 131, 135
Rolph, C. H., 24

Sarbin, T. R., 121
San Francisco Project, 125, 126, 130, 132
Savides, E. G., 185-8
Scottish Home and Health Department, 16
Selection for parole, 19, 20, 27, 28, 73-5, 99, 100, 109, 110, 118, 136-9, 177
Sentencing, 26, 31, 69, 81, 95, 114
Sexual offenders, 23, 142, 147, 153, 194, 195
Short-term prisoners, 25-7, 72

Skolnick, J. H., 120
Social enquiries, 42, 45, 46, 55, 77
Sparks, 123, 129
Special Intensive Parole Unit Project, 122, 124, 127, 128, 130
Springhill Prison, 52
Statistics of parole, 16, 18, 19, 22, 29, 52, 65, 88, 124-9, 132, 136, 137, 140, 142-4, 147, 149, 151, 153, 162, 174, 182, 183, 188, 189, 195, 197
Stonham, Lord, 74
Street, D., 119
Studt, E., 121
Supervision:
  duration of, 22, 25, 78-81
  of parolees, 18, 21-3, 25
Supervisory conditions, 18
Suspended sentences, 26
Sykes, G. M., 98, 119

Takagi, P., 113, 119, 126-8
Tentative Draft No. 5, 80, 82-4

United Nations Congress on the Prevention of Crime and the Treatment of Offenders, 58
US Federal Prison and Parole System, 120

Vacaville Institution, 186-8
Vere, P., 62
Violent offenders, see Dangerous offenders
Volunteer workers, 61, 62

Waldington, Lord Parker of, 26
Waller, I., 21
Wandsworth Prison, 52
Ward, D. A., 106, 121, 128
Warning letters, 92
Windlesham, Lord, 30
Work Release programmes, 179